Those Well Beloved Hills

The Happy Memories
of a
Yorkshire Man

by
Stephen Kirby

Edited by Martyn Kirby

Highgate Publications (Beverley) Limited
1986

© R. M. Kirby 1986

ISBN 0 948929 02 2

Published by
Highgate Publications (Beverley) Limited
24 Wylies Road, Beverley, North Humberside HU17 7AP
Telephone (0482) 866826

Cover by Jonathan Green Graphic Design
9 Marritt Way, Keyingham

Phototypeset in 10 on 11 point Times New Roman
and printed by
The Walkergate Press Limited
Lewis House, Springfield Way, Anlaby, Hull HU10 6RX

Preface

The great love of Stephen Kirby's life was Yorkshire, and this deep affection glows through all his stories of the people and places he had known. He writes with feeling but without sentimentality. His shrewd northcountryman's sense of humour kept his feet firmly on the ground but his gently lyrical descriptions recall the scenes which never lost their appeal. Martyn Kirby, his son, has edited this anthology of reminiscences which convey the happiness with which a Yorkshire man looks back with joy and gratitude.

John Markham

Acknowledgements

I gratefully acknowledge the *Hull Daily Mail* for allowing me to reproduce two photographs and Peter Braithwaite for permission to use photographs of his relative, Jim Dale. I thank the Duncombe Park Estate Agent who kindly gave permission for me to visit and to photograph *Antofts*. Some of the stories are similar to those first used in *The Dalesman* and *The Listener,* both of whom readily allowed me to include them in this book. I am indebted to Bernard Cattley for his meticulous work on the map of the Helmsley area and to Marjorie Whitton for her typing of the manuscript.

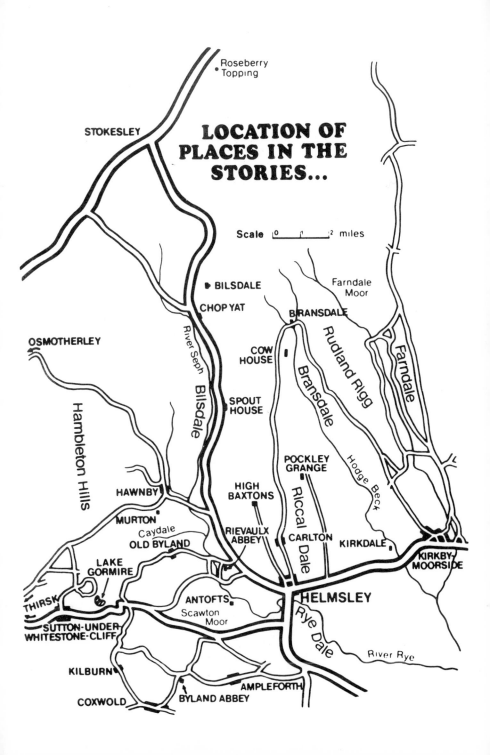

Roseberry
• Topping

STOKESLEY

LOCATION OF PLACES IN THE STORIES...

Scale 0 1 2 miles

▶ BILSDALE

CHOP YAT

OSMOTHERLEY

River Seph

Farndale Moor

BRANSDALE

COW HOUSE

Rudland Rigg

Farndale

Bilsdale

SPOUT HOUSE

Bransdale

Hambleton Hills

POCKLEY GRANGE

Hodge Beck

HAWNBY

HIGH BAXTONS

MURTON

Caydale
OLD BYLAND

RIEVAULX ABBEY

Riccal Dale

CARLTON

KIRKDALE

KIRKBY-MOORSIDE

LAKE GORMIRE

THIRSK

ANTOFTS

Scawton Moor

HELMSLEY

Rye Dale

River Rye

SUTTON-UNDER-WHITESTONE-CLIFF

KILBURN

COXWOLD

BYLAND ABBEY

AMPLEFORTH

High Baxtons Farm on the edge of the moor. Stephen Kirby was born here in 1895.

The road to the moor north of High Baxtons Farm.

The narrow winding lane to Helmsley from High Baxtons Farm. Between the ages of 5 and 7 Stephen rode his donkey down here to attend the school (now a private house) next to the gates of Duncombe Park Estate. His donkey was stabled at the Crown Inn.

Back to School

*The schoolboys mentioned in the following story were, like myself, at
Penshurst County Primary School at Hessle on the Humber bank.
Stephen was the first headmaster of this school when it was built in 1938
and he remained there until retirement in 1955. The description of him
then by a fellow headteacher as 'looking like a prospective contender for
Rocky Marciano's heavyweight title' was apt: Stephen had done some
boxing in World War I but was beaten in the army championship by a
certain 'Bombardier' Billy Wells.*

*The tiny moorland school he refers to is at East Moors, north of
Helmsley, and had been a single schoolroom joined to the master's
house only a few yards from the church of St. Mary Magdalen. The two
buildings are isolated on the moor among a clump of pines. Stephen,
aged seven, trudged the few miles over the moor from Pockley Grange
Farm for three formative years and was taught by John Tomline, a lay
brother trained at Mirfield, who looked after the church built to serve the
scattered community of moorland farmers. The National School, built
in 1888 at a cost of £400 to take 50 pupils, had a dozen or so in Stephen's
time and, according to 1905 records, had grown to 'average' 26 children.
Mr. Tomline's system of education stimulated this boy from a lonely
moorland farm so that, only a few months after the family moved to
Hooton Pagnell in the old West Riding, he became the very first scholar
of that village to win a scholarship to Mexborough Grammar School
where he later achieved distinction both as scholar and sportsman.*

When the boys of Form Four discovered the colony of ants in their
school garden they did me – their headmaster – a really good turn.
Unwittingly, of course. Tiny red ants these were, the kind of
determined little demons that work their way through the very
foundations of a house into the pantry to scare the housewife into
hysterics at supper time. Form Four's discovery really started
something, otherwise I might never have visited the moors that
summer. The lads adopted that colony and housed it in a glass-sided
box in their classroom, and a beautifully constructed affair it was,
almost like an observation hive. The things these youngsters collect!

7

Newts and lizards, worms and butterflies, beetles and moths – there's always a conglomeration of aquaria and terraria and jamjars and boxes littering up their room.

I ventured inside this classroom one hot summer's day mainly to suggest that a little more care should be taken over arithmetic. They hadn't done too well in the July examinations. But before I had a chance to introduce the topic I was side-tracked most adroitly. They drew red ants across the trail.

'Please, sir, have you seen them at work?'

'Don't you think Robson has made a fine job of this case, sir?'

'Don't take the cotton wool out of the plug hole, sir! Maurice did that yesterday and a dozen got away.'

It was very neatly done indeed. The case was almost a cabinet-maker's job, stained and varnished too. The ants were all hard at work, frantically making tunnels and chambers, carrying out a hundred and one vital tasks, scurrying about in the soil enclosed between the layers of glass. It was fun to watch them. Fascinating. In a few minutes I was completely absorbed and the lads bombarded me with questions. They knew my hobbies – and my weaknesses.

'You like our *formicarium,* sir?' asked one youth.

'*Formicarium*?' I echoed, taken right off my guard. 'What on earth's a *formicarium*?'

'Why, *this,* sir,' he said sweetly, 'this box for ants, sir. *Aqua* – water, *aquarium* – for water creatures; *formica* – ants, *formicarium* – for ants, sir. Teacher told us.'

He reminded me of Will Hay's star pupil and I looked upon him with distaste. Headmasters do *not* like being tripped up. *Formicarium* indeed!

For the next ten minutes I really let myself go – largely on the subject of ants. It was essential to re-establish myself. Luckily I do know something about these insects for when I was a boy I was brought up among ants, in a manner of speaking. In the pinewoods near our farm we had millions of them, and ant-hills of pine needles, hundreds of them, some four feet high and six feet across. When I studied ants I had no wretched *formicarium*!

To interest Form Four was no problem and I left them with regret, for I rejoice in their keenness for natural history. As to the exact length of time required to completely fill a bath with the cold tap and the hot tap running at different rates while the plug was out, did that greatly matter? Idiotic sums, many of them. When I got back to my study I looked through the window to a wilderness of slate roofs and back yards, while on the sultry July air came the smell of the fish dock. I thought longingly of the moors. What would I not give to be on that windy hill above Carlton, or down by the beck in Ricall Dale, or rambling over the heather past Pie Thorn towards the old Spout House? The breezes there were always pure, fresh, invigorating! Even the farm yard was preferable to this fishy odour.

That very Friday night I set off to Carlton. I just had to assuage that hungry, nostalgic longing by a visit, described by Uncle Arthur as 'coming back to get your bottle filled'. He was eighty-two years old and could always say the right thing. A kindly, courteous man, he loved that little village, as many generations of his forefathers had loved it. They were all farmers, honest to goodness yeomen, hard workers and keen horsemen. He sat a horse well, I remembered, and he cut a dashing figure in his full dress Hussar uniform as his troop of yeomanry clattered over the cobblestones in Helmsley market place. He looked equally well in cassock and surplice leading the church choir, and he presided with dignity at high tea when the curate was being entertained after service.

Forty years ago he played wonderful games with us youngsters; I could remember him taking all the local children on the annual outing to East Moors, four or five miles away. On that occasion his waggons were all shining and resplendent with new paint, his horses groomed to perfection and gay with ribbons and plaited manes and tails, harness all bright with jingling brasses which were the pride of his waggoners . . . and what hampers of choice food they loaded up for the picnic! Yes, he was a kindly man who held magic lantern shows for the whole village in his big kitchen before he managed to get the village hall built; a man who enjoyed a good song and approved of the piano and harmonium but who would not tolerate 'them squeaking phonographs'. How right his judgement was. The waggoner who produced a melodeon was commended as a musician but the lad who had brought a phonograph was told, 'Take it outside, me boy, and don't let me horses or cows hear it.' After half an hour with him I always felt better.

I halted at Cowhouse Bank Top and walked to the edge of the steep escarpment. The sudden revelation of the valley and moors down, far down, below is breathtaking. The brown waters of the beck gleam in the sunlight, the farms make a patch-work quilt of varied colours along the valley, and away to the north roll the purple moors and a grey thread of a road, beckoning the walker onward. I went down to the beck to the same amber pool where I paddled and splashed as a boy. The springy turf was warm in the sun, the beck beside me made music and the air was fragrant with summer sweetness. I watched the soft south wind rippling a field of barley like green satin. The whole valley was filled with beautiful summer. That night I slept outdoors beside the talking water. At peep of day over the moors the awakening birds among the alders roused me to the living world and after breakfasting I wandered on through a plantation of pines to the little schoolroom beside the tiny church. Through a cracked window I peeped in.

This tiny one-roomed building set amid the heather and pines was the school to which I went when I was seven, for we had moved to Pockley Grange. Time may steal the years away but the influence of that school stays with me to the end. I know how easy it is to parade a

The School on East Moor
The church is on the left. Near it is the master's house with its
adjoining schoolroom on the right.

sentimental affection for the distant past and to gloss over its defects, but I still say that I owe more to that little school high on the North Yorkshire Moors than to any other school I ever attended. There were seldom more than a dozen of us at that school, five-year-olds up to fourteen. A middle-aged bachelor with a bushy beard was our teacher and he 'ran' the little church close by. This energetic leader of our scattered community of 'Moor-enders' had no easy job, though he had one great advantage in knowing intimately each child and the parents too.

He certainly believed in a simple curriculum: it was reading, writing and sums, knitting, darning and sewing, for boys and girls alike. We absorbed a little history and geography from our general reading and when we were older we memorised dates and names of kings and queens, the chief rivers, capes and bays of Britain. We sang often and I can remember how occasionally we pushed aside the long desks and danced, while our master played jolly tunes on the harmonium. He always had the youngest child perched on the knee which went up and down as he pedalled. I suppose he was not a trained, certificated teacher but he certainly had methods all his own, and they worked!

10

The main feature was that the older children taught the beginners – and children are very often the most effective teachers – while he provided the rest with ample opportunities of self-education. He made us find out things for ourselves and insisted that we work. As for sums I remember working from pink cards such items as 115 tons 8 cwt. 2 qrs. 16 lb. of coal at £1.10.3d. per ton; I wrestled successfully with stocks and shares – not that I then understood what they were, nor have I had anything to do with them since. I dealt faithfully with baths that were filled by taps which ran water in at one rate and plugs which let it out at quite a different rate, though at home we bathed in a big zinc tub before the kitchen fire.

It was when we were not having lessons that our bearded teacher was at his brilliant best. He would take us into the garden to watch the bees at work, or into the woods where we learned about the trees, the birds, the flowers and the animals. We studied the life of insects in the heather, in the water and on the water. We learned from him good manners and polite speech, and the supreme importance of obedience. Because we were so few in number we got from him something very near to real education. He had a strong personality and its impact on me was a permanent influence.

We read extensively and there was a good supply of books which I fancy were his own private property. I read all Scott's novels, most of Stevenson's, all the works of Dickens. These were in rather small print, with very few illustrations. Then we had dozens of bound volumes of the *Boys Own* and even three or four great books called *History of the Crimean War,* in which I remember enjoying the dispatches of Lord Raglan and revelling in the gory details of *The Charge of the Light Brigade.* All was grist that came to my mill! Perhaps I owe him most for the way he introduced me to the world of books. He had an excellent library – no abridged editions written down specially for children, no hotch-potch collection of extracts, but the complete book. Admittedly some were poorly printed and badly got up, many had no illustrations, but the fact remains that I simply revelled in exploring this new wonderful world. Reading was never a lesson, it was an exciting adventure. I was hungry for books and he fed my appetite.

Each morning the two biggest boys went 'sticking', which meant collecting the daily supply of fuel from the wood. At mid-day the eldest girl made us cups of broth or cocoa; the stronger ones were taught to look after the weaker. For physical training we danced and skipped and climbed the trees – and some of us had two or three miles to walk home. Looking back I think I was fortunate indeed; I might have been brought up in a town with all the amenities of 'civilisation', one insignificant unit in a class of fifty, with a lovely tarmacadam yard to play in, well fenced in by iron railings.

Today the children from my valley go to school in Helmsley town in a taxi. It is no longer an economic possibility to keep the little school open; the older children have greater opportunities in a secondary school; all things considered it is the best thing to do. Mind you, if there had still been that little bearded schoolmaster in the valley today I would say that the children would be the losers if they left him. That little school was admittedly exceptional in every sense. The saintly character and impressive personality of a truly great man made it so.

Penshurst schoolchildren on their annual outing to East Moors.

The Cave in the Quarry

When I was a small boy one of my favourite playgrounds was a cave – a real cave that disappeared into the earth for a hundred thrilling yards. There was nothing 'pretending' about a cave of that size! Looked at from the outside you could see only a dark shadow in the face of the disused quarry. That was the entrance, a narrow one that caused even a small boy to crawl on his stomach in order to get inside; but once we had wriggled a few yards we could stand upright and explore the passages in comfort. We had then no electric torches but managed very well with bull's-eye lanterns. 'Jack, Jack Shine-a-Lights' we called them, and smelly things they were, burning oil. We wore them on our belts, and the fumes and smoke blackened our faces if we turned the wick too high. Still we loved them dearly and they produced wonderful shadows as we explored the dark, deep recesses of the cave.

Sometimes, before crawling inside, we would lie prone in the entrance and pretend we were men of the Stone Age, or Robin Hood's merry men, or highway robbers. We would sometimes defend our hide-out with bows and arrows, shooting down imaginary enemies. It was the best playground I ever had.

The little hole in the quarry face was about twenty feet above the quarry floor and the same distance below ground level. To reach it we would squirm along a narrow ledge and then pull ourselves up by a tree root or two. Looking out we could see the little valley of Kirkdale and between the trees we caught glimpses of the little church with the square tower. All round us were birds in the woods singing, and the music of the little River Dove floated up from the valley.

From that steep hill close by we might hear the dull rumble of waggons as great carthorses with jingling harness heaved and scrambled. Waggoners might shout and crack their whips to urge on their teams but we paid little heed to anything except the cave. All that was fifty years ago, and since then countless numbers of small boys will have played there. Even my grandfather did so when he was a lad, soon after the cave was discovered.

In 1821 a young student on holiday at home in Helmsley was walking in Kirkdale when he came upon roadmen spreading stones on the highway near St. Gregory's Minster. He stopped for a chat and

13

happened to notice, lying among the stones, a considerable number of bones. 'Them? Oh, they're just cattle bones, I reckon,' one of the men told him. 'I've dug heaps of 'em out of t' quarry. Happen there was a cattle plague in t'owden days and they dumped dead animals there.' The young student was studying geology and the bones intrigued him so much that he there and then collected a large number of specimens and next day he gathered more, then sent parcels of them to various eminent authorities for their opinions. One of the parcels went to Dr. Buckland, a celebrated geologist at Oxford, and so excited him that he caught the first available coach to York and from there another coach took him to Kirbymoorside. That same evening he scrambled up the quarry and crawled into the cave which the student had found. He realised at once that a really great discovery had been made – a discovery that would excite the whole of England! The entire cave and its contents must be examined with the utmost care, he decided, and gathered together a party of workmen.

They dug away the soft mud from the floor of the cave, and below that they found, embedded in the harder dry mud, great quantities of bones. The cave throughout its hundred yards or more was littered with the remains of thousands of dead animals.

The rock there is limestone, and from the roof water has dripped down through the ages, bringing with it a fine deposit that covered up the bones so that they were still undamaged when Buckland took them out. He examined every tiny fragment until the entire cave was cleared, a job that took several weeks. What a tremendous collection of bones! It was a fascinating task to classify them all, but when Buckland had done so he had the complete bones of over three hundred hyenas, of several elephants, of two sorts of rhinoceros, several mammoths, sabre-toothed tigers, lions, hippopotami, bears, wild horses, bison, elk, red deer, reindeer, wolves, foxes, even the tiny bones of mice, watervoles and birds.

Buckland's discovery excited the whole scientific world and proved that these animals had inhabited our island in the pre-historic era. His fame as a geologist rests on this momentous find. The Royal Society awarded him its highest honour, the Copley Medal. Two years later he published a full account of his work at Kirkdale and I read this with much interest in the reference library at Hull. He had been most thorough in his investigations and took great pains to prove his statements. For example he spent some time at Wombwell's menagerie to study the habits of their hyenas. 'I found their jaws exceedingly strong,' he wrote, 'like a miner's crushing mill, or those scissors with which they cut off bars of iron or copper.'

Then he visited the Zoo in London and gave the hyenas there the time of their lives by feeding them with the carcasses of horses, sheep and oxen in order to study what they did with the bones. He noted how they cracked them to extract the marrow and the exact way they piled the bones on the floor of the den. He took the bones and examined them carefully for marks made by the hyenas' teeth. He compared those marks with the marks on the Kirkdale bones and found them identical. Only then did he decide that my cave had once been a hyenas' den. In most of our large museums you can examine bones from Kirkdale Cave, though I believe Hull lost its collection in the air raids on that city. York's Museum in St. Mary's Abbey gardens, so I have been told, was built specially to house the many specimens given to it by Dr. Buckland.

I was at Kirkdale not long ago with my youngest son and naturally we crawled inside the cave. We had an electric torch and a ball of string, one end of which we tied to a projecting root outside the narrow entrance. You can quite easily get lost in the various passages. There's still the constant drip, drip of water from the roof, so the floor is soft and muddy. We saw no bones of course; they all went in 1821. But we did see many footprints, smallish ones, though not the distinctive prints we used to make, with toe plates and heel plates and hob nails. At any rate there was ample evidence that small boys still play there, but I doubt if they use bows and arrows, nor will they know the thrill of wearing a bull's-eye lantern.

The remains of Kirkdale Cave

I was the small boy in the story who explored the cave – re-creating the exploits of Stephen some 40 years previously. The main cave entrance no longer exists, having been excavated to leave a flat floor open to the

15

air, but travellers can see a letterbox slit on the cliff face just large enough for a small boy to investigate.

One of the many interesting letters in Stephen's scrapbook is from Sir James Shelley who said that his visit to Kirkdale with Stephen had been 'the most outstanding spot of a most delightful tour . . . among your beautiful dales'. The story of the cave was included in The Listener in 1945 following a radio broadcast. This was one of the earliest of Stephen's many radio talks about his beloved North Riding moors.

St. Gregory's Minster, Kirkdale.
Above the main door is a famous Saxon sundial with inscription.

My Gallant Grey

The old photograph comes out every Christmas to stand on the mantelpiece among the greeting cards. It's a trifle faded and dog-eared, which isn't to be wondered at since it is now over fifty years old. My wife stands it there each year. It was the first Christmas greeting I sent her, back in 1914 when I was a trooper in the King's Own Royal Regiment of Norfolk Imperial Yeomanry, camped in the mud at Rendlesham Park in Suffolk. It pictures me at eighteen, standing proudly beside my beloved grey charger, Seagull.

Most of our troopers were farmers who had brought with them their own horses but we recruits were marched off to the horse lines and given a mount from the collection of requisitioned horses. They all seemed useful animals but the one I fancied most was a grey, a really handsome horse, just over sixteen hands. He looked to me the pick of the bunch and I guessed he'd be able to show a clean pair of heels to any horse in the lines. Timidly, as became a raw recruit, I asked the sergeant major if there was any chance of my having him. 'Seagull, the Grey? He's one of Lord Woodhouse's hunters, I believe. Somebody has to have 'im, so it might as well be you, me lucky lad.' I thanked him warmly and fancied there was a sly grin on his face as he turned away, but I was too happy to give much thought to the sergeant major. Seagull and I soon loved each other. Whenever I had a few minutes to spare I would be over at the horse lines, petting him, slipping him a little extra corn, grooming him till his coat shone like burnished silver. A wonder horse he certainly was and he could jump like a stag. When I rode him round the park he made most of the other horses look like hacks.

It was not till we went off on manoeuvres one brisk November day that I realised why the sergeant major had grinned when he let me have Seagull. We had galloped down a wide green lane with infantry firing blanks at us, then my troop halted in a hollow. That is to say, they all halted save Seagull and me! He seemed madly excited, snorted, pranced and jogged me violently up and down, then took the bit in his mouth and away he went, flying over the hedge and racing across the field! I managed to stay on and pulled and tugged with all my might, but there was no checking the big grey and we went straight ahead over hedges and ditches till we finally slowed down in the middle of a sixty-acre field that had recently been ploughed. He stopped and tossed his head, then turned round and we jogged slowly back to rejoin my grinning comrades. They chaffed me unmercifully for days.

Fortunately I soon discovered the cause of Seagull's strange behaviour. When we rode to the water troughs, or took our horses out for exercise, we used our 'spare saddlery' – privately provided equipment with nickel-plated stirrup irons and snaffle-bits so that our regulation kit could be kept smart. On all such occasions Seagull was the best-mannered charger in the troop and responded at once to the slightest touch of the rein. 'That's it! He hates the bar bit and the ruddy curb,' I thought; then I fitted a light snaffle bit to my regulation bridle and all was well for a few days till there came a 'snap' inspection by the brigadier. The trumpeters sounded 'Boot and Saddle' and we formed up in quick time. My own troop was the first to be inspected and the fierce-looking old man halted before Seagull, glared at me, then bellowed, 'What's this? What? Gad, Colonel, damme it's a SNAFFLE.' His retinue of aristocrats gazed at me sadly. The colonel was purple in the face and my troop's lieutenant was as white as a sheet. I half expected to be tried by court martial and shot next dawn! Later that same day I did my best to explain my conduct and the colonel let me down lightly with, 'Seven days C.B. and see that your damned horse gets trained to wear the proper bit.' Poor Seagull. Henceforth he had to suffer the torment of bar bit and chain curb.

By gentle handling we managed to avoid further trouble for a few weeks. I talked to him and never let him feel that wretched curb. Then came the memorable day on Martlesham Heath when the entire brigade, eighteen hundred cavalry, was put through a series of exercises by the Brigadier. The grand finale came late in the day. Norfolks, Suffolks and Welsh Horse, all in line, heard the trumpeters sound the thrilling notes of the 'Charge'. We thundered across that heath going hell for leather, swords flashing in the sunset, men and horses mad with excitement. A few horses went down where the ground was tunnelled by rabbits, but Seagull was sure of foot, tough and sinewy, the ideal charger. His neck was outstretched, his ears laid back, he was certainly enjoying this! This was his idea of heaven, this was a race! I felt him lengthen his powerful stride. This was, he decided, a race that he must win. In a few minutes we were yards ahead of the troop.

Reins in my left hand, sword outstretched in my right, my body lying forward, I had no earthly chance of checking him and we swept on. The bit was in his teeth and all I could do was to ride on, a helpless, cursing passenger. We galloped past captains, past majors, past the Colonel and even past the furious Brigadier. Oh boy! What a ride! What a ride to remember! It was not long before I realised with a sinking heart that we were both for the 'high jump'. Poor Seagull! From that day forth he was condemned to the indignity of pulling a transport waggon, yoked alongside an ugly animal of lesser breed. I had a lump in my throat whenever I saw him thus ill used.

'All that a horse should have he did not lack,
Save a proud rider on so proud a back.'

To replace him I was given a clumsy black with huge feet. He had probably pulled a cab in his heyday. I endured him only a few weeks, for our horses were taken from us and we sailed to Gallipoli as foot-sloggers, though they called us 'dismounted Cavalry', and later on we wore a broken spur as a divisional emblem. Sometimes we would sing:

'My charger lies over the ocean,
My charger lies over the sea,
My charger lies over the ocean,
Oh, bring back my charger to me.'

Many a time I would think of Seagull and wonder how he was faring. I had kept a note of his number and identification particulars and when the war was over I wrote to the War Office, hoping for a chance to buy him. They replied that he had been killed in action.

Even nowadays, half a century later, 'in vacant or in pensive mood', pictures of Seagull flash upon my 'inward eye'. Surely some intelligent officer would restore him to the rank of charger . . . maybe he would have been ridden in a charge against the Turks in Palestine. I can picture him on the battlefield, galloping way out in front, sure enough, with his neck outstretched and his ears laid back and the bit between his teeth.

So, in affectionate memory of the finest horse I ever rode, the photograph of the pair of us comes out every Christmas to stand among the greeting cards.

Bilsdale – my magic land

When a North Riding exile is dreaming of home I wonder what picture he sees? The hills, of course! Some deep-cut dale, a rough grey ribbon of road that lazily trails through the heather, a cluster of houses, stone, sturdy and grey surrounding the church on the green? The scenes may vary, but my own nostalgic dreams are always of some quiet spot high on the northern moors. When my dreams come true and I can stand alone, high on some windy hill to look around, the actual sight is far more lovely than the dream. The colours are much richer and the air is filled with fragrance; there's the potent spell that's woven by the wind amid the trees; there is birdsong and the honeyed hum of summer. There is, best of all, just knowing that the picture cannot fade.

Once, when my dream came true, I found myself beneath a group of pines, wind-blasted trees that topped a cliff-like edge near Sutton Bank, and somewhere near a thousand feet above the Vale of York. A few brief days on that flat plain below are always quite enough for me. Sometimes I stay with relatives down there, stroll with them round their rich, fat lands, admire aloud their bumper crops and herds of grazing cattle, but frankly it is what the French call *'politesse'*, impatiently observed. The plain truth is that in a week or so my eyes will wander northward and my feet persist in itching. Then soon I murmur an excuse, though no one is deceived, and off I go hot-foot towards the Hambletons or Clevelands or the Moors where I belong. If ever things go wrong I know for certain that solace and satisfaction can be found among the hills. The very moment that I cross these untrodden tops and feel the wiry heather spring beneath my feet I am a brand new man.

Happiness just comes seeping in with every kiss of wind and rain – there is much more than 'gold in them there hills'. Down on the plain I often find myself a little irritated at the sight of their squat, trim roadside edges and the neatly carved ditches alongside them, and I dislike their smooth tarmacadam roads with streams of traffic dashing madly hither and thither all day and half the night. Give me the narrow, grey, rough ribbons of roads that go alone and unattended, roads that wander carelessly uphill and down dale, roads that a man can stride along, singing as he goes, where grouse and curlew and black-faced sheep are the only critics of his voice. Woe betide me if I sang on the roads in the suburbs where I live.

As I stood and stared from Sutton Bank Top I leaned against the winds that sweep so strongly up the slopes of Hambleton – the winds that flow over Sutton-under-Whitestone Cliff and little Kilburn village. These are the winds that lift the gliders up the sky and howl away eastward by Cold Kirby and Old Byland. And from this height I stared down on almost half of Yorkshire, spread below me like a map. In the far distance I saw the blue outline of the Pennines, and in between lay a score of towns, hundreds of villages and many thousands of tiny fields, all clear and fresh in the sweetness of a May morning.

There were woods, bedecked in every shade of green, and amid the trees misty acres of bluebells, while great patches still remained of dead, golden-brown bracken. Gleaming like a great jewel lay Gormire, a lake framed in an emerald meadow; and seeking in vain to climb the cliff-like edge on which I stood and stared, a carpet of primroses. To the south I could see the three towers of York Minster. Although nearly twenty miles away the great church appeared like a galleon in full sail riding across the Vale of York. To the north lay Darlington and through binoculars I watched an express train crawl steadily from there southward to the City of York. Just round the edge of Roulston Scar was the White Horse of Kilburn, famous landmark of the Coxwold country. Below it nestled Kilburn village, famed all over England through the craftsmanship of my old friend Bob Thompson, who worked in English oak and on each lovely piece left his trademark – the little mouse as a sign of industry in a quiet place.

A man with field glasses and a map could spend a whole day above Sutton Bank, but I turned my face to the east and tramped over to Wass by the bridle road, and on to Byland Abbey, lying so snug below the southern ridge of Hambleton with its sprawling ruins that indicate the immensity and grandeur of the Abbey as it once was. I must have explored it a score of times, so I passed by. I trudged along the Old Drove Road – the self-same road along which, even in my grand-father's time, vast herds of lowing bullocks lumbered to and from the north. On this high track following the crest of the hills the Picts and Scots came down to plunder, and in its time it echoed to the tramp of Roman legions. Today it has in parts been metalled, but for the greater part remains a grass green lane and one of the most delightful tramping roads in Yorkshire.

For a few miles I strode on springy turf between lanes of golden gorse towards High Paradise. What's in a name? Not far from this farmstead is Low Paradise, named I suppose by someone who decided that one was 'not Paradise enow'. It was there I met a farmer whose main interest appeared to be racehorses. 'Best gallops in England up 'ere' he declared, 'and best turf. Air up 'ere brisks 'osses up tremendous.' It appears that in the 18th century Hambleton was the Mecca of the north for the racing fraternity. Coaches toiled up Sutton Bank, then steeper than it is today, bringing the nobility and aristocracy to the classic race, *The Hambleton Guineas*. However, when ladies began taking an interest in the sport, accommodation on the hills proved inadequate and the fixtures were transferred to Richmond and later to York. He pointed out the racing stables and told me tales of various great horses, one an unrideable white mare. 'Nobody could stop on 'er back more than a few minutes, but a new jockey came on t'scene and vowed he'd ride 'er if he rode 'er to the devil.' The horse was blindfolded, the jockey lifted into the saddle. The cloth over the mare's eyes was pulled off, then away she went. Her rider, faithful to his vow, was not unseated and away galloped the white mare and over the cliff-like edge they 'flew like a great eagle, doon and doon inti Gormire Lake and were nivver seen agean.'

I walked down to Old Byland village, the site of the original Abbey. It was because the bells of Rievaulx clashed with those of Byland that the two Cistercian communities were at loggerheads. The Byland monks finally flitted to a new home on the other side of Scawton Moor, to build their much more magnificent monastery near the village of Wass. From Old Byland down to Caydale I hurried, for I knew of old how delightful that secluded little dale is, with the old mill still there beside the river. I climbed to Murton and had a marvellous view down my beloved Ryedale, and then on to Hawnby village, surrounded by great hills and glorious woods – the village where the annual sheep sale is so great an event. Soon I came to Bilsdale.

When I sat beside our cowman on the granary steps at High Baxtons those many years ago he would often describe the wonderful world that lay 'on t'other side, yonder past that pine wood on t'sky line.' Over there, he said, lay an enchanting valley twelve miles long, a tumbling beck winding along, teaming with trout and grayling. There was a far-famed pack of hounds that hunted the biggest foxes in England. There were hills and dales more beautifully patterned than Grandma's best embroidery. The very names he mentioned had a ringing music – Bumper Castle, Chop Yat, Hollin Bower, Bracken Hill and Spout House.

Then when he wanted to give me a thrill he would tell stories of a witch who turned herself into a hare and enticed the hounds away, far over the heaving wastes of moorland, across surging streams and peat bogs right to her little stone house into which she vanished through a hole in the wall. Then when the raging huntsman arrived to collect his hounds he would enter the house to discover she was back in human form again, 'liggin' doon on t'sofa, puffin' an' blowin' an' all of a lather'.

In all my life I have never yet met his equal for strange lore and weird superstitions, and he believed every word he spoke. My grandma vouched for most of it too, and even my mother could not bring herself to dismiss it all as fairy tales. As for me, I would jog along home on my donkey after school when the evening mist hung low over the moorland road and times out of count I would see the toothless grin of 'Old Peg Humphries' in many a larch tree root. She would change into a giant here before my very eyes and make off, licketty-spit, across the heather to East Moors.

So Bilsdale became for me a veritable magnet. Yet, try as I might, nobody would find the time to take a small boy across the gullies and becks that crossed the intervening moorland. After being persuaded once or twice by means of a leather strap not again to set off alone I never did get there till years afterwards, for we moved to another farm when I was seven.

Stephen at 14, was now a pupil at Mexborough Grammar School. He was visiting his dales for a holiday at the time of the cattle drive.

It would be when I was fourteen, a leggy lad in corduroy breeches and hob-nailed boots, that I first clapped eyes on my valley. I was spending a week with an uncle, a cattle dealer, and he sent me off with my cousin Jim to drive some twenty bullocks from Harome towards Stokesley. There were two of us boys, both about the same age, and we were provided with a sheep dog, a pony and cart, bullock walloper's sticks, a basket of eatables and sixpence each to spend.

We whacked and shouted and barked our lumbering way through Helmsley market place and climbed steadily upwards towards Rievaulx. As we toiled on I grew steadily more excited, for the old cowman's magic was still with me. Every thwack on a laggard bullock's flank brought me nearer, and when at last we reached the top of Newgate Bank I saw the whole beauteous length of the dale bathed in sunshine. The heather hills stretched away into the purple distance; the peaty river Seph sparkled below, far below in the valley; the blue smoke curled upwards from the grey stone houses. I found myself gulping and blinking and Jim thought I had a midge in my eye.

'You shouldn't open your ees so wide,' he said, screwed up his handkerchief and hunted for the trouble.

'Nowt there!' he decided. 'Let's be off. Git on Rover. Send 'em on!'

So we rolled away down the hill and in due time handed over the bullocks to a drover from Stokesley who met us at Spout House, our old cowman's favourite inn. We dined by the roadside, spent our money on dandelion and burdock and then rode back in the trap 'down to England' as my cousin said. He was an unromantic lad who poured scorn on my few outbursts of enthusiasm. 'You're makin' a lot of fuss about nowt. It's a'most a wilderness up here, can't call this good feeding land for cattle.'

My next visit was after the First World War. Back from the Somme I was utterly weary and with some vague notion of becoming a farmer I went to Bilsdale Show. I chatted with the dalesmen, prodded sheep and looked knowingly at cattle. I rejoiced to see Canon Kyle, 't'owd farming parson', driving his pair of cart-horses in the show ring and congratulated him on winning so many prizes with his sheep. To mix with country characters all laughing and joking nineteen to the dozen really did my heart good. I almost became a farmer there and then.

So I came again on that May day, to sample again the sweetest air that ever filled human lungs and quickened the heart. The hills seemed a trifle hard against gathering storm clouds, but Bilsdale remained as exquisite as ever. There were many more umber patches of ploughland but the patchwork of fields and woods was mapped out sharply, outlined by stone walls – just the same shamelessly romantic picture as it was when I was fourteen. I longed to settle down there at once and have done with the world. Then suddenly, down came the rain, whereupon I sought shelter in the Spout House.

Mine host was then William Ainslie who not only managed the inn but farmed 150 acres and was huntsman of the famous Bilsdale Hounds. When we met he was a little worried. 'They're selling this dale', he explained. 'Aye, the whole bag o' tricks, twelve or thirteen thousand acres and I'll admit we're all in a bit of a sweat about it.' He wasn't concerned about his tenure, that was safe enough, but about the hunting. 'I nobbut hope somebody will turn up wi' plenty o' brass and buy it all in one lot. I want to see nowt happen to the freedom of this dale.'

Freedom is many sided, but in this case he meant liberty to hunt without let or hindrance – something very dear to the hearts of men of Bilsdale. It is part of their heritage, and they claim that theirs is the oldest hunt in England. It was the sporting George Villiers, second Duke of Buckingham, who founded the hunt and he was the hardest rider in the dale, their genial companion who spoke their dialect and entertained the followers liberally at Bumper Castle – a farm where he kept a very good cellar. In London the profligacy of his private life was notorious and he was banished from Court. He therefore came to his castle at Helmsley, threw himself whole-heartedly into enjoying the pursuits of a country squire and became the first Master of Fox Hounds of a moorland pack. 'T'Owd Duke – he were a reight proper man – liked his joke an' his glass and knew a good hoss when he saw one.' So, after three centuries his name is still used affectionately. His brilliant wit matched their own rough humour; his generosity at Bumper Castle gained their friendship and his horsemanship won their admiration. They showed me 'Buckingham's Stone', a slab in a plantation which still marks the spot where one of his hunters fell dead during the chase.

The hunt was managed by a committee, with mine host of the Spout House as huntsman and secretary, and he told me that in the current season they killed twelve brace of foxes. It was not unusual to hunt from 9.30 in the morning till 10.30 at night. Their total expenses were in the region of £120 a year, for the hounds were trencher-fed. Back in 1865, when my grandfather was an active supporter, the yearly budget was a mere £6.2s.6d., which included such items as '8s. for the Hunt Supper, 2s.9d. for getting hounds out of jet mines, 10s. to John B. for rearing young foxes', together with minor expenses for collecting hounds from very remote farms on the day before hunting. They still keep the original type of hound – a light-coloured breed very like the Cumberland packs.

For no less a period than sixty years ending in 1902 they had a huntsman named Bobby Dawson and today his name is spoken with reverence and his fame increases with the years. In my talk with William Ainslie I happened to mention that foxes were being shot in some parts of England and was promptly told, 'My goodness! Bobby Dawson wouldn't have liked that.' It appears that a certain local gentleman who had suffered considerable losses through foxes gave his gamekeeper orders to shoot a fox. Bobby went to see him and the fur began to fly. 'Ya know, ya've educated that there keeper o' yours up tiv it. When he dees (*dies*) Ah'll spit on his grave. And when Ah dees, Ah'll seek him oot no matter how yat (*hot*) it is, and Ah'll pull him by t'lug into t'yattest part Ah can find – and that won't be half yat enough!'

When Bobby died the dalesmen decided to furnish a grand memorial stone in the form of a cross. On it was carved a fox's head, a brush, and a huntsman's whip, and the epitaph read:

'Sacred to the memory of Bobby Dawson,
Sixty Years Huntsman of the Bilsdale Pack.'

With due ceremony it was taken on a horse-drawn waggon to the churchyard, with all the hunting fraternity in attendance. The vicar met them at the gates, took a look at the cross and told them with very great regret that it could not be put into the churchyard – it was a pagan memorial and the ecclesiastical authorities could not possibly allow it. There was great consternation at this, but they understood their vicar's position, and held an emergency committee meeting at once in the lane.

Spout House (Sun Inn) in Bilsdale. To the left is the old thatched inn.

'Owd Bobby were varry fond o' t'Spout House,' someone said. 'I propose we erect it there.' This was agreed upon with much enthusiasm and the memorial stands today in the front garden, facing the high road. It amused me to learn that soon after its erection there was a protest made because of an important omission from the epitaph. So they added this to the inscription at the base of the cross:

'And also wicket-keeper of the
Spout House Cricket Club for many years.'

I know of no district where people cling more closely to tradition than in Bilsdale. It is not unusual to find families who have held the same farms for three or four hundred years, some even longer. William Ainslie told me that his family had held tenancy of the inn in unbroken succession of Williams for at least five hundred years.

We chatted about the 'freedom of the dale' and wondered who

*Bobby Dawson's cross which
stands at the front corner
of the Sun Inn.*

might be the next owner. Many dalesmen were making arrangements to buy their farms if there was a chance. The forthcoming sale was the main topic at the inn. 'We'd like somebody to come along and buy Bilsdale in one lot,' they told me, 'but he'd better be a good sportsman.'

A few days later I dropped in to the sale. They were all there, these farmers, a trifle self-conscious perhaps in their Sunday suits, grave of face, talking solemnly among themselves in hushed voices. A property sale is by no means a jovial affair, there are no quips such as we get at farm auctions, no rustic humour, no colour, no bellowing cattle or bleating sheep or prancing horses. It is all very much more like a family lawyer reading out a will to expectant, sad-faced relatives. There is, however, the same tense expectancy in the air.

This sale was no exception. The low room was crowded to such an extent that I was admitted with some difficulty through a window and squeezed into a seat near the front. Catalogues rustled and there was a scraping of chairs as the auctioneer rose to his feet. 'Bilsdale, twelve thousand acres! Three villages, one hundred and five farms, moorland, shooting and fishing rights, all in one lot!' Bidding began at £40,000. It rose rapidly in big advances, but it petered out at £95,000, and the auctioneer shook his head. It was then put up in lots, each farm and little property separately. Inns, farmsteads, cottages, small holdings, the village school – bought and re-sold again immediately for the Red Cross at a hundred guineas – the whole dale was disposed of in three hours, every acre, every house for somewhere near £130,000.

In nearly every case the tenant farmer bought the property which his family had farmed for so many generations. The innkeepers now own their own inns and they bought them to vociferous rounds of applause.

Masters in their own houses, innkeepers and farmers, they left the sale well content, happy in the knowledge that the future of their beloved dale was settled. So Bilsdale goes on unchanged, to me and to many others the loveliest spot in the loveliest part of the North Yorkshire Moors.

Cold tea, apple pie and cheese provided welcome refreshment for hard-working harvesters.
(Photograph loaned by John and Enid Bulmer).

Hedger and Ditcher

The narrow by-road to the farm climbs steadily over the moor to the solitary clump of pines, then dips steeply down to the valley. Just round the pines you emerge from a desert of heather, suddenly brought face to face with a scene of rare beauty. From our imposing vantage point we looked down on the loveliness of the dale. Vociferous amber becks writhed and twisted amid sloping pastures backed by heaving heather hills. I glanced enquiringly at my wife. 'Oh, it's wonderful,' she breathed. 'I'd no idea it would be like this.'

It was well over thirty years since last I stood there. The saplings of my boyhood had grown into giant pine trees, but little else – save for one red-brick bungalow – had changed. 'There used to be a short cut – ah, there it is – through the wood and across the river. Takes you straight as a die to the farm. Like to walk it? You would? Right! Mother and I will drive round – maybe there before you.'

My son and daughter raced away while I free-wheeled the car for a mile or so till we reached the beck. The rickety footbridge was still swaying and my wife walked across it to open the gate beyond the ford. As the engine started up, blackfaced sheep scuttled nimbly off, then ambled cautiously back to look at us. Dogs in the distance began barking, each taking up the cry from his neighbour till the whole valley was filled with alarm. I felt an intruder, rudely destroying the peace of this September morning, so I stopped the engine and stood on the grass, waiting. Soon the sounds all died away and the valley was still.

'Hullo there, mister,' said a deep voice. I spun round. If a gun had exploded I couldn't have been more surprised, for not a soul was in sight.

'Hello to you,' I said. 'Where on earth are you?'

''Ere,' replied the voice.

Then a huge leather mitten appeared through the hedge beside me, to be followed by an old fellow in an indescribable tweed cap, tattered corduroy suit and a straggly grey beard.

'Sorry if I startled you a bit,' he said. 'You makin' for the Low Farm I reckon.'

'The very place.'

'Know yer road?'

29

'Yes – I know it well enough, thanks.'

'Mm, ye do? Well, this 'ere used to be the road, wi' hoss and trap. But it's no use for motors. Smash yer springs like as not, an' besides you've the beck to cross again – be two foot deep at least – 'appen three.'

Of course it would be. How stupid of me not to have thought of that. But then I'd never crossed it in a car thirty odd years back. But that old chap's voice . . . it was deep, musical almost. It reminded me of somebody, somewhere.

'Perhaps you'll be kind enough to tell me the best way,' I suggested.

'Easy enough – you passed the new road a couple o' gates back.'

I thanked him. Now whose voice *did* it remind me of? I *had* heard it before. I must hear it again.

'Hedging I see.'

'Aye – just liggin' (*laying*) this bit o' rough,' and he waved his mittened hand while his eyes gave me an invitation to inspect his handiwork. I promptly accepted. I love to see a well-laid hedge.

'That's a grand job you're making of it,' I said. It was certainly a brute of a hedge to tackle.

'I like to mak' a tidy job,' the old craftsman replied. 'When I were a young chap we had a feller frev Leicestershire way as were a reight champion hedger – aye, he taught me a thing or two about laying a hedge. But that's a while back, he'll ha' been dead this forty year.'

'Why, you'd only be a youngster then. You don't look more than sixty now.'

'Seventy-four,' he announced proudly, 'an' nivver a single day off work in sixty years. How's that for hard work and fresh air? Mind you, I've only been a hedger and ditcher this twenty year – afore that I were a hired hand – cowman mostly.'

I stared at him. Cowman? Why, of course! Then, slowly, I asked him.

'And how about that leg, Billy? Does it ever bother you nowadays?'

It was his turn to stare. He peered steadily from under his bushy brows for fully a minute. 'Why now, you're no stranger,' he muttered to himself, 'you're fra' roond here, I'll bet a sovereign. Aye, you're a Moor-end chap really, but I can't ken ye.' Then walking closer to me he said, 'Let's have a good squint at ye. Noo let's have ye sideways on! That nose o' yours – that's it! I've got ye taped – you've gotton t'owd family nose! Eeh, lad, I owt to ha' known ye straight away. We saw a lot of one another when you were a nipper,' and he gripped my hand. It was touching to see the light of recognition in his old eyes and to feel the welcome of his horny fist.

We stood there chatting of days long since gone by till my wife reminded me of the children. Billy almost danced with delight when I told him of my boy.

'T'owd family nose'll nivver die oot,' he declared.

We laughed and turned to go.   '

'See you again, Billy, then we'll have a reight long crack about old times. We're stopping for a few days.'

'Come doon toneet!' he cried eagerly. 'Meet me doon 'ere by t'bridge, say eight o'clock sharp.'

I shook my head, but he continued to plead.

'It happens I've summat special on toneet. Let's meet 'ere at eight! Do, just for old time's sake, like. And bring your laddie wi' ye.' I agreed and was getting in the car when he added, with a wink, 'Strong boots an' owd clothes is best.' It wasn't till I had driven well away that I realised what the old scoundrel meant.

The original 'Billy' is here on the left. Colin is standing in front of the other countryman.

When we reached the farm the children were already very much at home. My daughter was in love with the kitchen, and no wonder. They still had the floor sanded, while hams hung from the dark oak beams, and warming pans, muskets and yeomanry swords adorned the walls. Her nine-year-old brother was enchanted by an enormous meat pie on the table. It was a thrilling experience to revisit this old place after so many long years, to explore the old haunts. Somehow the trees I used to climb didn't seem quite so high, but it was delightful to take my family around, proving to them that my bed-time stories were, at any rate, founded on fact.

It was dusk when Colin and I set off to meet Billy, and as we skirted the woods I began to feel a trifle uneasy. Here was I, a middle-aged, highly respected townsman, occupying a prominent public position, taking my nicely brought-up son to a rendezvous with a wicked, though lovable, old rascal who was, even forty years ago, the most accomplished poacher in the county and the despair of every gamekeeper and village constable for miles around. As we neared the beck the stars came out and the moon climbed over the wood; the night was comfortably warm and the air almost still. 'Step softly now,' I whispered. 'Don't talk aloud, and watch carefully.' So we padded along in silence, save for the rippling of the stream and faint rustlings among the dead leaves in the hedgerow.

'Idiot!' I called myself, 'to bring the child out – and fool for coming yourself,' and I was in two minds about turning back. But I pictured past moonlight nights with Billy, then a pheasant called in the distance and I hungered again for the thrill.

'It'll do the lad good,' I said to my other self, so we stayed, waiting.

But where *was* the old rascal? I looked up and down and we walked to and fro on the springy turf, but there was no sign of him.

'Maybe we're early,' I whispered, and as Colin held up his new watch to the moonbeams its ticking sounded alarmingly loud.

'Two minutes past eight, Dad,' he whispered back, and slid his watch back in his breast pocket.

I was bending down to tie a boot lace when an owl hooted close at hand. We both jumped. Then I discovered the old man at my elbow, chuckling at having crept up unseen.

'Just like his dad was,' he said. 'Hunny, you're the spitten image of your dad when I first took him in hand. Now then, old Billy's going to take you both for a lovely little ramble. Eeh, but it's grand to have you with me – and it's a wonderful night for a bit o' sport. Bobby's away on point duty at York races and keeper's over on t'highroad side. Still, Billy ain't taking no risks, so you've gotter stick close by me and mind you don't step out o' t'shadow. Still as mice and silent as the grave, as your grandfather used to say.'

Few men knew the woods and their inhabitants like Billy, and as we crept along he whispered interpretations of every rustle and sound. Now and then we halted to inspect snares, cunningly set by day across runs in the hedgerows.

'Doesn't it hurt them?' asked Colin, as Billy took the wire from the neck of a dead rabbit.

'Bless you, no. I never causes hurt to no dumb critter. This 'ere sniggle, the way I sets it, kills master Bunny in less than two ticks o' your new watch. Now, you see how I sets 'em, like this. That's the way it's done. But I'm none leaving sniggles around for them keepers to see.' We hid half a dozen rabbits and two hares, and the snares, in a hole in the hedgerow – the very one he was laying in the daytime. 'Farmer Jackson pays me a pund a chain for that there hedge,' he chuckled. 'I can't get over rich at that price, so I reckon the old hedge owes me a bob or two.'

Hugging the shadows we climbed steadily up to the wood. Billy halted now and then to listen. Owls hooted once or twice; lights flickered palely at the lonely farms and the headlights of a car making for town swept like searchlights over the moor. Across the pastures drifted the sound of a concertina and singing. 'Farm lads a-tuning-up in t'stable afore they turns in for t'neet,' Billy explained to my son. Then we entered the wood. Silence brooded like a living, watchful thing over the sleeping valley, bathed in bright moonlight. 'Months since I were up 'ere,' Billy whispered. 'I mostly keeps to rabbits nowadays. Still, I must show t'lahtle lad how to use a bit o' hoss hair in the light of the silvery moon,' and from his back, beneath his coat, he took out a small bundle of thin canes and fitted them together to make a long flexible rod. To the end of it he fixed a noose of horse hair.

On we crept, deeper and deeper into the wood, while the shadows grew blacker. Billy glided ahead, silently, halting, listening, trying the ground for random twigs before stepping further. I heard not a sound save our breathing. My son's hand in mine grew hot and sticky with excitement. Then Billy stopped and beckoned us to join him. Pointing upward he showed us the birds outlined against the moon – black as jet. Up went his rod, there was a dextrous flick of the wrist, a noiseless flutter and the pheasant was lowered. It found a home in his capacious pocket. 'Better 'n potting 'em wi' a gun, that,' he whispered. 'It don't even waken 'em out o' their beauty sleep.' And down came another. 'That's lesson number one, and now, how about a bit o' ferreting?' Colin danced up and down in gleeful anticipation.

Billy's coat was just one vast pocket and from it came the nets and Jerry – a pale yellow ferret with red fiery eyes flashing in the moonlight. We pegged down our net and away went Jerry underground. 'Now then, me hunny, put your ear down like this an' listen to 'em,' came the order, and I could watch the delight in Colin's face when he heard the subterranean thumping, a scurry, and then, like a flash, the rabbit dashed into the net! It was fascinating to watch the old man at work – the sudden flurry, a quick grab with the left hand, a downward chop with the right and that rabbit joined the pheasant in less time than it takes to tell of it. We listened again to Jerry. Suddenly Billy stood upright and so did I. Through that burrow I heard, magnified a thousand fold, the tread of heavy feet approaching.

'Keeper! Blast him,' hissed Billy. While he recovered Jerry I gathered up the net. Then we glided deeper into the wood and stood motionless, waiting, listening.

33

Here was a nice situation! I could already see the headlines in the papers, the request of the Governors for my resignation, the acid comments of the magistrate, my wife's face. What a fool I was!

'Happen he'll pass by in a minute or two.' For three or four minutes – which seemed like half an hour – we stood like statues behind a holly bush. But the keeper did not pass by, and the footsteps drew nearer and nearer. I held my son close as we crouched down. He was shaking – with suppressed laughter. This was *real* fun – to him. Then the keeper halted. I peered anxiously round our bush and saw him standing in the moonlit clearing, listening, obviously a trifle suspicious. Then he sat down on the trunk of a fallen larch, took out his pipe and struck a match, while we remained in hiding only fifty yards away – motionless. I have never known a pipe of tobacco last so long. Then, as we crouched, an agonising cramp seized my left leg. I stood up and Colin followed suit.

'Snap!' went a dead twig beneath his foot. The keeper put his pipe away and stood up. The moonlight gleamed on his gun barrel. He strode rapidly towards our holly bush.

'Stay put – I'll deal with 'im – you get back to t'highroad,' whispered Billy and melted away in the shadows. We 'stayed put' holding our breath, though the keeper was less than twenty yards away.

'Crash!' went a branch – a splintering crack over in the wood. The keeper turned and went off at a run. Dragging Colin by the hand I headed in the opposite direction for the road to freedom. It was only a quarter of a mile, but dodging trees and bushes made it heavy going. In the distance came yet another crack from a breaking branch and I heard the faint echo of a voice, 'I'll get ye, ye divil.'

When we reached the fence I was wringing wet with sweat, out of breath, speechless. I was too old for this sort of exercise. Then I remembered that Billy was nearly twice my age. Poor old Billy – never been caught before in all his long life of poaching! It would break his old heart. Still, first offence, they'd only fine him and I'd gladly pay that. Soon I recovered my breath, mopping my streaming face and took out a cigarette.

'Dad, why can't we make some sort of row, like Billy did?' asked Colin.

'Why not?' and I put my fingers to my mouth and produced a piercing whistle, then another, that set all the dogs on the dale a-barking. We walked boldly along the road, then stopped to listen. The clock in the church struck ten. Talking gaily, laughing and joking we stamped along, then burst into triumphant song. We had just reached the middle of a rollicking chorus when the keeper stepped out into the road. He was panting and his face gleamed wet in the moonlight.

'Good evening!' I called out, cheerily.

He grunted and looked closely at us. Then, 'Evenin' sir,' he said. 'You're the gentleman I seed at Low Farm this afternoon. Couldn't make out who it was at first.'

'That's right,' I said. 'You've been running?'

'Aye, I have an' all. Ruddy poachers! I heard 'em plain enough, can't see how they've got away. Did you hear one of 'em whistle a bit back?'

'I should think we did,' I replied. 'A very shrill whistle it was too. It sounded back over there somewhere. Difficult to tell at night.'

'Thank you, sir. I'll have a look over yonder,' and away he went.

'Goodnight,' we called together, then resumed our singing and stepped out smartly down the road. I had to shorten my stride just a trifle in order to keep in step with my partner and to fit the rhythm of the song. We had just finished our final:

'Oh 'tis my delight on a shiny night
In the season of the year,'

when we reached the gateway to the farm. And there, leaning contentedly on the gate, puffing away at his clay pipe, consuming his own special mixture of coltsfoot, clover and twist, was Billy, admiring the stars overhead, his upturned face as innocent and guileless as a child's. His pockets were flat and empty.

'Eeh, but it's a lovely neet,' he said, 'best neet we've had for many a bright year. And I liked your bit of singing – that were a nice little hymn. Now I think we owt to try my favourite,' and his deep voice rolled out:

'I saw the old 'omestead an' faces I loved,
I saw England's valleys and dells,
I listened with joy as I did when a boy
To the sound of the old village bells.
The moon was shining brightly
Twas a neet that would banish all sin . . .'

He paused. 'Aye, summat like tonight, I suppose, just real good fun; a night that has banished all sin. But we mun away to bed. Good neet, hunny, I hope you enjoyed it.'

Postscript:

When we left the farm after that week-end, I discovered in the boot of my car a brace of pheasants and a hare neatly wrapped in sacking. Incidentally the attractive hat now being worn by my wife is adorned by some very fine feathers. They were certainly very fine birds.

The Harvester

An all-conquering September sun had swept from the moors the last flimsy veil of morning mist when my wife, my two children and I left the car. Down, far down in the valley, amber waters foamed and bubbled as the beck played hide and seek among the alders. Heather and pine scented the warm air. Toiling bees shook the heather bells, the trees whispered, the grasshoppers chirruped loudly in the purple floor beneath a sky serenely blue. The singing birds were no gayer than the four of us, as we raced down a track amid the pines, dodging, leaping, laughing, on a springy carpet of brown needles. Presently we heard 'tlot, tlot,' of horse's hoofs on the nearby road. A rider on a dales pony jogged loosely towards us, astride the world's most dilapidated saddle. He had a careworn expression, a straggling moustache, and a crop of untidy hair beneath a battered hat. We strolled to meet him.

He touched his hat and dismounted with a, 'Fine day, sir.'

'A lovely day,' I agreed.

'Grand,' he said. 'I ought to ha' been on cutting.'

'What? Corn?' I asked. 'Surely you're a bit late? There's not much corn left standing as late as this.'

He nodded.

'Generally a month behind, up here,' he explained. 'I'd have "downed" it all yesterday, only t'old binder went wrong.'

I sympathised. It was an ideal harvest morning. 'Barley?' I asked.

'Best crop I ever had,' he replied, 'but it's "necking" and another day or two'll waste it. I came to meet blacksmith and carry his tools. It's two miles across t'moor, and over rough for a bike. Happen you passed him? Little chap, he'd have a box of tools on his handlebar.'

'Not a soul for eight miles,' I told him. He looked crestfallen and bit his nails, then took another look down the white road.

'Deng him!' he cried. 'T'lubber can't be coming after all. Bit o' corn'll be ruined.' He turned to go. 'Deng him!' he growled again, as he climbed up on the pony.

I felt downright sorry for him. After all, no real countryman can bear to see good corn spoiling.

'Here, wait a minute,' I said. 'Maybe I could do something to help. I've lots of tools in the car.'

He thanked me kindly, but his eyes looked full of doubt.

'Binders is tricky things,' he warned me, 'and you'd get yourself all mucked up.'

I smiled. 'I don't mind a bit of dirt,' I said, and that seemed to cheer him up a little. I expect we looked the very essence of Town, but a drowning man will clutch at a straw. The youngsters produced the tool-kit by that, so we set off, my boy astride the pony – his feet in the leathers, and the rusty stirrups dangling – with his sister striding alongside. We others walked through the heather beside the deeply rutted track in silence. I waited for him to speak.

'Know much about binders, sir?'

'Depends,' I answered. 'What sort is it?'

He named it – a type well-known thirty years ago. 'Not much in my line I'm afraid. But we'll have a look,' I told him. It isn't policy to know too much in the country.

'I don't understand 'em,' he explained. 'Only bought it last April at a sale – but I'm relying on that bit of corn for rent in October. It means a lot to me does that barley, and *this* weather won't last.'

'Any one to help you?'

'Only t'missus,' he replied, 'and she's not what you'd call strong.' I sympathised, for I knew what a struggle it was on those out-of-the-way farms, tucked away in the back-of-beyond. We turned in through a gateway in a stone wall, and the glory of the harvest lay before us. Now, I find a harvest field just as charming today as I did thirty years ago, in spite of modern appliances. But here, on the moors, time had stood still, and the old binder might have been the very same that I knew when a boy. I looked at it, enchanted. Walked round it, as in a dream.

'Three hours steady cutting, and you'll down what's left,' I told him. He stared at me, wondering maybe. It was obvious that he was no mechanic, and the briefest examination enabled me to advise him to fetch his horses. While he was gone I patched up the job, and, according to my daughter – who is rather particular about appearances – the prophecy that I might get 'mucked up' was amply fulfilled. Binders prefer a plentiful supply of oil, and this old model was smothered in grease. We yoked the pony alongside a heavy carthorse of very uncertain age. 'Samson and Delilah' my wife named them – for the pony was a mare and the giant had a blind eye and Roman nose. With a clanking and a jerking the ancient machine rolled forward; the ripe barley fell to the canvas, and, with rhythmic clanks that told me all was well, the neat sheaves pitched regularly to the stubble.

It was a strangely satisfying sight, that rusty old contraption reaping the swaying corn. With a sigh I turned and walked away, for we were due to lunch at Whitby – two hours' run at least. But the clattering and clanging suddenly stopped, and we looked round. Beside his machine the dalesman stood, once more despondent, scratching his untidy head.

'Gone again,' he said when I reached him. 'I told ya they were tricky things.' I opened my tool-kit again.

'Dang that blacksmith,' he muttered.

'Got any split pins?' But he shook his head.

'Then fetch me some nails and a washer or two,' I ordered, and he went off to the house. I could tell that he no longer had much faith in me.

Rummaging among the tools I came across the very things tucked in a corner; but he was out of ear-shot, so I got on with it and fixed all up a second time.

'Tricky things!' I snorted. 'I'll show him,' and I climbed up to the seat. It was a queer sensation to be up on a binder again. I felt like a last-wicket batsman, out of practice but the only hope of his side. I took up the reins and lifted the whip from its socket.

'Swank!' said my daughter.

'Go on, Dad,' piped my son. 'Show him!'

'Careful,' warned my wife.

'Giddup!' I shouted, and shook the reins. Samson and Delilah responded nobly, and we shuddered along once more, just as the dalesman re-entered the field. But I'd no intention of stopping – my blood was up. I fetched Samson a vicious cut across his ancient quarters.

'Did this thirty years ago!' I shouted to the children. They yelled back, but the rattling drowned their voices, and the vibration of my insecure perch made my teeth chatter, and jerked my spine from end to end. Still I felt a king! The sails swept round, stroking the satin heads to the canvas; the barley disappeared, to be thrown noisily forth into regular rows of sheaves, as my royal chariot rolled along.

'Blow the lunch!' I said to myself, as we came to the edge of the rectangle. Samson stepped lumberingly sideways, while Delilah sidled mincingly across, and we clanked into position for the shorter side.

'Gerrup there,' I shouted. 'Gerron, Samson!'

Little Delilah went at it without urging.

The farmer caught us up and climbed on the step to shout in my ear. 'She's not TYING!' he yelled. So we stopped.

The last score of sheaves were lying loose.

'Tools!' I snapped to my boy, and he scuttled off across the field.

Till he returned we tied up the sheaves. The sun poured down, the air was almost still, and great clouds of flies pestered the patient animals. I threw off my coat and collar and rolled up my sleeves.

'We must have it cut today,' I told him. 'Rain might be here by tomorrow.'

'They're tricky things, these old binders,' he said. I made no reply, although I was beginning to agree with him. Then I found myself automatically twisting straw bands, tying with my right hand, slinging the sheaf away and jerking out enough straw for the next.

'That's proper Ryedale fashion,' remarked the farmer. 'Where'd you pick *that* up?' But I got busy on the machinery without an answer. That corn *had* to come down, no matter how tricky the binder might be.

'Fetch my pipe from the car,' I said to the children as I put away the tools.

'Better let 'em tell my missus you're stopping,' said the dalesman.

'That's about it,' I answered, and mounted to the iron seat. I packed a few handfuls of straw on it, then clattered and clanged away.

Slowly, steadily, the central patch became less and less, though times out of count we stopped for repairs. Every nut that wasn't rusted on seemed to have shaken loose; and at each successive halt the sultry air betokened rain – and ruined corn.

But it came at last, that triumphant turn to sweep up the last tapering strip of standing grain, and like a conqueror I halted amid the cheers of two young voices. The farmer looked pleased as he paused in his stooking.

'My word, you've mucked yourself up proper,' he said as we freed the lathered horses of their collars. I staggered towards my coat.

Then his wife and mine appeared carrying baskets and a great can of tea. No lunch that Whitby ever provided could equal the rabbit pie, the mugs of hot tea and the bilberry tart eaten on the edge of that stubble field. We thanked each other, and then the clouds appeared. Was the rain going to ruin my labour after all?

'We ought to get it in,' I said. 'It's bone dry.'

'The missus and I can manage I think,' said our host, but, poor woman, she didn't look fit to be forking corn. So we stayed, joyfully determined to see it through. The children roamed the fields and paddled in the beck where the sheep were dipped, while we men carted home to the barn load after load of booty. By tea-time half of it was safe, but the sky looked menacing.

'We mustn't leave one single load,' I said.

'Very near all me corn was rotten in t'field last year,' said my partner. 'Maybe rain for a week when it does start.'

I borrowed a pair of gloves, for my hands were raw and bleeding where the blisters had been. I felt ashamed of them – soft and white, letting me down; and ashamed that my back was fit to break and that my shirt was wringing wet with unaccustomed sweat. It would be eight o'clock when the cart rumbled back for the last load, with the sky so overcast that it was almost dark.

'Think I'll loaden this one,' I said – the truth was that I could fork no longer. I just hadn't enough strength left to throw a sheaf up to him.

'Good old Dad,' cried my son, who was riding on Samson. 'Show him how to do it.'

Boastfully I said something about putting on a *proper* load this time, as I started laying the first course of sheaves. Now, loadening isn't quite so simple as it looks, and by the time I slid down the rope I felt a little doubtful about the result. But the last sheaf was on, and we roped her tight enough, for the road was rough. But I must confess that the load was badly made, and we entered the yard with the two of us holding it on the cart with our forks – an inglorious end to a triumphant day! Then, on the very threshold of the barn, Samson stumbled slightly, and then, like the house of the Philistines, the load collapsed about our heads.

'Swank!' said my dutiful daughter.

'Good old Dad,' said my son, helping to pull barley horns out of my scanty hair. Wearily we tossed the sheaves under cover, washed, had a hurried meal, and rode back to the car in the heavy cart, blissfully tired and well-content. The harvest was home.

The engine purred and we drove off just as the lightning flashed and the first great spots of rain came down.

'Best day I've had for years,' said my son aged nine as the deluge began.

'Same here,' I told him. 'Say goodbye to the farmer.'

'And you can say goodbye to that suit,' said my wife, 'and who's going to get that oil and filth off your shirt?'

A horse-drawn binder of the period.
(From a photograph loaned by Jim Dixon.)

40

Uncle Seth – Auctioneer

Seth Kirby – the auctioneer

It's simply not possible to be a passive spectator at a sheep sale on the Yorkshire Moors – the dalesmen see to that. They have the problem of coaxing reluctant flocks into the field amid all the clamour of men, dogs, motor vehicles and shouting boys, and they very properly demand that ungrudging assistance of every bystander. Moor sheep are much wilder than March hares. Picture me, lazily leaning against a gate post, musing on the serene beauty of the valley that nestles below the rounded hills near Bilsdale. The village of Hawnby, the moorland beck, the shaggy woods, the towering rims of heather-clad hills – these all seem to welcome a wanderer home.

'Hi there!' yelled a sweating farmer. 'Lend a hand will ya? I want them perishin' gimmers *(unshorn sheep under two-years-old)* into pen twenty-fower. 'Ere, turn that yan! You chaps that eats mutton owt to be able to help us chaps what provides it, instead of propping up a gatepost.'

So I tried obediently to hustle his wayward flock into their specified enclosure and when they were at last crowded therein, panting, head above head, I was told, 'Thank ya, and now, if you will, I've two more lots to fetch – I can't stand gossiping here all day, so let's get on with it.'

Every lane in the vicinity seemed choked with vehicles – lorries, tractors, creaking tub traps, horses and carts, cars of every vintage with the most amazing collection of trailers, and even a sledge or two. Sledges can travel easily across the heather and may save miles of road.

Here and there were dalesmen on shaggy ponies or thick-set cobs and, as was to be expected in this sporting country, a few farmers on hunters. But most conspicuous of all were boys and dogs – they seemed to be everywhere – and the noise they made passes belief. It exceeded in volume the bleating of the few thousand sheep now assembled in the pens. There were bustling farmers' wives, clean and neat, and rosy-faced with the excitement of it all. There were even a few land girls in their attractive slouch hats and green jerseys – and not far from them a few soldier lads home on leave, for this visit of mine to the sheep sale was in 1944. One could pick out the inevitable dealers by their long brown coats, overalls and bowler hats. But most of the adults were obviously farmers, browned, healthful and strong: rather untidy in their working clothes and with dogs at heel and sticks that worked overtime.

Now every dales farmer has two dogs, a pipe and a stick. Dogs and pipe have obvious uses but the stick is an instrument of very special advantage. It props up the tired frame, it supports the chin, it hooks selected sheep from the flock, it drives on the backward and turns the wayward, it emphasises an instruction to the dogs, signals bids in the ring, waves greeting to a friend – but it is used primarily for the very vital procedure of prodding. What dalesman can estimate properly the value of an animal without first pushing back his cap, cocking his head aside and prodding the creature gently? After a studious jab you'll hear the verdict, 'Nice ewes them. Happen fetch forty-five apiece.' Further along the row of pens you may see a lad of twelve lean knowingly across a hurdle, stick in hand, and he'll say, 'Um! Nobbut a middling lot, them. Shouldn't like to give more than thirty apiece for 'em.' You might even see our local doctor using his cane like a stethoscope; and the parson is sure to be there too, stout ash plant in hand, reminding one of his flock that the baby's christening will be at 2.30 on Sunday and poking away at his ewes as he says it.

As the pens fill up, the crowd grows. What a jolly crowd it is too. There's a spate of greetings, crude neighbourly banter and here and there roars of laughter.

'That'll be old George tellin' 'em t'tale – my, but he can stretch a yarn can old George.'

It's certainly an *event,* this annual sheep sale, with the school closed and the local pub open all day. But beneath the jollity one senses competition, tense expectation and relentless rivalry. It only needs a referee to step into the ring and one could well imagine that a prize fight was about to begin.

And here comes the master of ceremonies, waving his stick and bellowing greetings right and left. He strides up the slope, swaggering a little maybe, like some great actor, conscious that he alone holds the stage today, playing the leading part as he has done for fifty years.

42

'Fresh as paint, though he's seventy summat,' they say to each other.

'Aye, he takes a bit o' beating does Seth. None of them young 'uns can hold a candle to 'un.'

'Now I'm afraid he's failing a lahtle bit,' says another. 'He hasn't brought his 'unting 'orn, can't be giving us t'*View Hallo!* today. I remember time when you could hear him two – three mile off. And sing! My goodness, he could liven 'em up at rent dinner with his *Fine Old English Gentleman*. But let's be up t' ring, he's a'most ready for selling.'

The buyers cluster round and the owner stands ready to let his sheep out of their pen. Then Uncle Seth clears his throat, waves his stick aloft, and calls, 'Gentlemen!' in a voice that fills the valley. Even the boys stand still.

'All's in *H*order, gentlemen! A'll's in *H*order!

Time's time, we must be getting *H*on!'

The very sheep cease bleating and scarcely a dog whimpers. Then he bellows, 'Let 'em *H*OUT, William, let 'em *H*OUT!' And the first dozen or so of black-faced sheep come under the hammer.

'I shall not dwell, gentlemen, I shall not tarry! Time's time, can't dilly-dally! Grand lot o' sheep here – can I say forty-five? Forty-five anywhere? Forty I'm bid, at forty, at forty-five, at fifty shall I say? Fifty I'm bid – going at fifty shillings apiece.' Then smack went his stick. Bidding was brisk and his patter as compelling as a machine gun.

It amazed me how he spotted the bids for one man might merely raise an eyebrow, another nod almost imperceptibly, another lift his stick a few inches, or flick a thumb across his coat collar, or tap a hand on his stick. There are dozens of surreptitious signals, for it seems part of the game to conceal any intention of buying. But he knows what to expect, for he took bids in exactly similar fashion from their fathers and some of their grandfathers before them. The poker-faced buyers know that he can read almost their very thoughts.

One young fellow came in with his sheep and said behind his hand, 'Shan't let 'em go under thirty-eight apiece.'

'Then you'll take 'em *H*out! Take 'em *H*out and SHARP!' roared the grand old man. 'They'll never fetch above thirty-six,' and '*H*OUT' they went amid the appreciative grins of the crowd. He stands no nonsense. A little later they sent in a veteran ram with great curled horns, probably well past his prime. The crowd chuckled.

'How much for this fine old gentleman? Lots o' life in him yet! Who says thirty shillings? His horns are worth that for hat racks. Finest hat racks ever seen! Twenty-five then – gimme a start, gentlemen. Let's be getting *H*on.'

'Ten,' said a voice. There was a deathly silence.

'TEN!' roared Uncle Seth. 'Did I hear TEN? The man that said that should have ten years! It's an insult to this fine old gentleman. For only ten bob – going at only TEN – take him home, sir, ride him out hunting! I think I'll hand over my hammer after that – my son will now take *H*OVER!' And away he went down the hill for a little refreshment while the auction went briskly on. The son was business-like and efficient enough, though he lacked the showmanship of his sire, and I wandered away to mingle with the crowd at some distance from the ring.

Below us in the valley the blue smoke of turves of peat curled upward from a score of chimneys of stone cottages – a reek which is to me much more than an attractive scent. It took me back thirty years or more when I was a lad living not far from here. I like nothing better than mixing with a crowd of 'my ain folk' and hearing them talk. Snatches of trivial conversation delight me, though my town friends find the dialect a problem. In this way I learned with glee that Harry had decided to marry one of the Land Army girls. 'Strong as any man,' they said. It would seem quite a saving of brass too, for he could sack his housekeeper and get a grand landworker into the bargain. They nudged one another and pointed her out.

'Happen Harry isn't as fly as he fancies,' said one philosopher. 'That lass'll mebbe alter a bit when she's wed. She's none weak in t'head isn't yon lass. I'll lay you a pund that she'll be running the farm afore they're wed a month.'

Another group was discussing the damage done to the road by the great timber-hauling waggons.

'Ruts!' said one. 'I've nivver seen nowt like 'em; they're two – three foot deep down our land.'

'That's nowt,' said another. 'You should see ours! I was coming home fra' market last Friday and there was Jimmy Dowker stuck fast in one – nobbut his head and shoulders above ground like. D'ye know, I got off my hoss and went to pull him oot, but could I heck as get him up. "What's holdin' you, Jimmy?" I says. He looked up at me and he says, "I've gotten me blooming feet fast in t'stirrups."'

In another corner they talked of the Bilsdale Hunt.

'I meet 'em one day, top of our hill and I stops to talk. Maister axed me if I'd seen ony foxes about. I told him it would nobbut waste time looking for 'em so he axed as why. "You prints your meet in t'*Malton Messenger*," I says. "And what's that go to do with it?" he says. "Why it's like this," I says. "I were up here yesterday an' I seed a great big dog fox sitting on that stone. He were reading *Malton Messenger* and laughing his blooming 'ead off, so you can all get off hoam."'

It appeared that the new hand at one farm wasn't entirely satis-factory. 'I set him on to sweep t'yard yesterday, and when I went out later he'd nowt much to show for an hour's work. "Broom keeps comin' off'n t'handle," he said. He hadn't half finished when I seed him two hours after that. He were standing again t'barn door looking fair flummoxed. "Has t'broom head come off again?" I said. "No," he said, "but blooming handle's been comin' offn t'head."'

Then came a great bellow from the veteran auctioneer, a hush among the gossips and a surging forward to the ring where Uncle Seth was waving his stick. 'Red Cross, gentlemen, Red Cross! I'll not allow any one of you to miss this lot, so dig down in your breeches' pockets and bid up! There's not a lubber among you who can't afford five bob and dozens of you can afford five pund! A five pund-note is nowt to some of ye! Nowt! And let me remind you what you all owe to good seasons – grand weather these last two years. The Great Author sends you the rain and the sun! Remember that! Now be generous in this grand cause. This pen of ewes – six grand 'uns – let's get HON! Five shillings apiece now and you'll put 'em in again?' Up went a forest of hands, while he rattled off their names like lightning. 'Now they're in again – a grand lot these at forty apiece, at forty, at forty-two, at forty-four, forty-four, at forty-five apiece only offered, gentlemen, these ewes have been GIVEN for the RED CROSS and you bid me a miserable forty-five! At forty-six, forty – seven, fifty. I'm bid at fifty! Can I say fifty-five anywhere?

He hammered on the rails till he cracked his stick, upbraiding, persuading, preaching little sermons on the virtue of generosity till he had drawn the uttermost pound, till there was no one left who would 'put 'em in again'. It was a rattling performance and the crowd loved being made to surrender their brass. That'll be Hall, gentlemen, that'll be HALL! It's not enough but it'll have to do. Pay in the office as fast as you like – THEY want to be getting Hon!'

When the hammer fell for the last time the boys and dogs became vocal again, accompanying the departing sheep and spectators. There was hustling in the temporary office where the buyers settled up, there was bustling in the kitchen of the local and for me a hasty meal in a farmhouse with the auctioneers. They gave me a lift across the moors in the fading light. Tired flocks were being driven to fresh pastures and our progress was slow, for sheep had to be moved off the narrow roads to let us get by. It was indeed a charming picture, flocks winding 'softly along the road of evening in a twilight dim with rose,' but Uncle Seth was in no mood for poetry.

'Come on, drover! get 'em out of me road!' he thundered. 'I've summat to do tomorrow. Let's be getting Hon!'

45

The Deerpark on Scawton Moor

Deerstalker Jim Dale

*Jim Dale holding the antlers
of a netted stag.
(From a photograph loaned by
Peter Braithwaite).*

Deerstalker Jim Dale had a mighty poor opinion of my eyesight.

'You townies are half blind; you never see nowt but bricks and mortar. There's ten or a dozen deer on yon slope and you reckon you can't see 'em. There man – in a line wi' them larches, betwixt the two patches o' bracken; and nearest the skyline there's a fine stag for you. A royal – a twelve pointer – dang it all, you can't help but see him; why he's nobbut a mile off.'

We were knee-deep in heather, in the shade of a clump of larches on one of the highest points of the North Yorkshire Moors. Over the many acres of deerpark flowed a gentle wind, rustling the ling, waving the bracken and making music in the larches, a scented, invigorating breeze like wine. From our vantage point the wide expanse appeared to be a plateau of heather dappled with bright green pools of bracken, but actually it is slashed by deep ravines – 'ghylls' in this district – all running down to the river. Down, far down in the valley, there's the River Rye playing hide-and-seek among the alders. Nestling below the wood at the distant bend is Rievaulx Abbey and away over the other side of the deerpark is the sister abbey of Byland. In the opposite direction we get glimpses of the Wolds.

Rievaulx ('Rie Vale') Abbey seen from Scawton Moor.

Jim Dale had been wise enough to stick to his heritage and for forty-eight years he was in charge of the herds of deer. In his seventieth year he looked little more than fifty and was as fit as a fiddle – 'wick as an eel' he would say. 'It's fresh air an' hard graft an' plenty o' venison what keeps me on me toes, man. You townies – you get heavy neets and light stomachs.' Like most countrymen he talked at length of the good old days when 'things were summatlike', for they had a thousand head of deer when he first started, in two separate herds, red and fallow. He lamented, 'Today we've nobbut a few, aboot two hundred an' fifty, all reds.' They were a hardy lot and would soon increase if not systematically thinned out. So from August to February, apart from a few weeks in the rutting season, they shot a selected number of stags and hinds, each one over eight-years-old. They are not venison if they're younger.

'You should ha' been here in May or June time,' said Jim. 'Then there might ha' been summat you *could* ha' seen. I could ha' taken you up a calf or two.' He never called then fawns. The hinds dropped them as a rule in the deep bracken and he often came across a newly-born calf and made friends with it. Indeed the little creature might become so affectionate that he had quite a job to get rid of it. 'Mind you, if a calf has once supped its mother's milk it's not a tame 'un. It would be up and off like a hare, and by gum, it would tak' a fast dog to keep up wi' a calf that's a day owd,' he explained. 'Why, I've known 'em nobbut five hours after being born follow t'owd hind over two mile. Then she'd leave her calf in hiding and the cute little beggar stops crouched down

47

flat, just like a rabbit. Then when danger threatens she dashes up to it, says, "Come on," and away the pair on 'em go like lightning. And she knows just how far t'little 'un can gallop – a mile, mebbe half a mile. Then she stops and strikes it down and goes on alone. You'd be mighty clever if you could find it, but if you did happen across it you'd see it crouched flat, but ready for off like shot outer a gun.'

In my ignorance I asked if the hind hurt the calf when she struck it down and Jim gave me a pitying look. It's a deerstalking term and implies nothing more than touching it with her nose. As we talked the dozen head of deer on the slope must have sighted us and crossed the skyline. They were gone in a flash, but I did get a grand silhouette of the twelve pointer.

'How old is he, Jim?'

'Ten.'

'And what will he weigh?'

'Twenty stone.'

I thought that was pretty good judgment, with the stag a mile off.

'That's nowt,' said Jim. 'I know 'im like a brother.'

I made a remark about his antlers and Jim cut me short.

'If thoo'd ha' stopped in this quarter thoo'd not have been so ignorant,' he said, shaking his head sadly, and explained that a male has a horn like a tiny knob in its first year, but in the second year it grows larger – like pointed spikes. In the third year they have two or three points, or tines, or antlers, and these increase in number and become more branches up to the seventh year. After that the horn from which the antlers grow becomes thicker and stronger.

'You townies!' he snorted. 'Why, I've had 'em come here, them fellows that writes books, an' they don't even know that a stag's horns drop off every year. They fall off about April time, and if you'd been here a bit earlier you'd have seen their new horns in the velvet. That means the horn is covered with summat like a velvet skin, an' it's so tender it can't bear touching. If it got a knock it 'ud bleed – its full of bloodvessels. But it sort of dries up and then the velvet comes off, and the horn's hard and ready to use. Eh, but it is a comical sight to see a couple of stags having a scrap when their horns are in velvet. They daren't use 'em, so they stand right up on their hind legs and slash away wi' their forehoofs, just like a couple of fellows boxing.'

There are many ferocious duels in the mating season. In Jim's words, 'They're allus scrapping, and you should hear 'em roaring, just like lions. They'll slash each other to ribbons aye, kill each other, all through some little chit of a hind.' He said he has known them fight till they've got their horns interlocked, and he's had to get them free. It usually means sawing them apart. It also means roping the pair and manoeuvring them to a tree till the operation's done. Jim is also a skilled tracker, an art which enables him to hunt down a wounded animal or one which has escaped from the park. He thinks nothing of it after serving seven-times-seven years' apprenticeship at the job, though he did confess that he sometimes had trouble in getting an old stag who had learned all the tricks of the trade. These veterans sometimes leave the herd and live alone, lying hidden in the deep bracken by day and coming out to feed by night. To get *him* our deerstalker is out at dawn or dusk, to catch him as he leaves the lair. He may stumble across an empty lair, but, should he set foot on it, it will never be used again. 'It's nowt, deerstalking,' he said. 'All you do is pick out a deer, crawl like a snake to a decent range – 100 or 500 yards – then bowl him over. It's no use letting him see you, or he'll soon be miles away and you'll start all over again. So you just wriggle along – see that the wind is right road on so he won't scent you, and put a bullet through his heart. It's nowt much.'

And this veteran can still stalk his quarry for six or eight hours over many miles of the roughest country, as part of his day's work. If he drops the deer in an awkward spot down a steep hill-side where his cart can't get, he takes the old pony and drags him out. Then when he gets him home he's to be skinned and dressed and cut up into joints. Jim has a tidy butcher's shop at home. He served his apprenticeship as a butcher specially for this job. I was surprised to learn that deerstalking was so many-sided and that deer were profitable. I'd always imagined that stag-hunting was an expensive amusement. 'Nowt o' t' sort,' said Jim indignantly, 'They take no rearing. They only need a bit of hay now and again in bad winters. They'll always scratch down for moss and such like, and they live up on the moors where nowt else could.'

We descended to Jim's commodious stone house, snug on the side of a ravine in the very heart of the deerpark and looking out over lovely Ryedale. We admired his spotless butcher's shop, his black pigs, his poultry, and envied him the orchard, the view and the singing pines and larches. But I certainly did not envy his trips to market in winter, for I remember what snowdrifts are like up here and I've heard tales of the perils of crossing the Rye in flood. It's a tricky job negotiating that ford. I suggested to Jim that a second-hand tank would suit him after the war, but his reply was pungent; I gathered that he preferred the old galloway – that's his pony.

I remembered that I hadn't tasted venison pasty since I was a small boy. So I decided to go to Jim's market stall on the Friday to try my luck. They give preference to the estate workers, then to the tenants, and the general public comes last, so I had faint hopes. Jim told me I was 'nobbut an outligger, like.' That's what they call deer that have got out of the park. There's about 15 miles of fencing and walls, all 6 feet high, but still there's an odd one gets over occasionally. They fancy another pasture and don't know when they're well off. Then they've to be tracked and shot.

When market day came I soon spotted his stall – he'd a laughing crowd of countrywomen with baskets listening to his backchat; and the spotless boards were piled with joints of venison. No cashier ever had a busier hour than his assistant and no butcher sold meat more smartly than Jim Dale. Clad in his snow-white coat, knife in hand and steel dangling at his waist he looked the complete butcher. 'Like a bit for roasting, missus? Just as you like it – this'll either roast, boil, fry or pie,' and he slapped it on the scales. 'Four and half pounds – not too much? I should think it isn't. Where you been all morning, Sally? Stew this bit and you'll be up earlier of a morn – this'll put you on your toes. Two shillings. Next?'

I wondered if I might have just a little . . . 'All right,' said Jim. 'You've waited very patiently and you're nobbut pasty and white. You must have a decent meal for once. King's dish at a poor man's price. Three pounds for five bob.'

In that busy hour the stall was emptied save for a deer's heart. There was a bullet hole, slap in the centre . . . and then the heart, too, found a customer. As we left I asked Jim how he liked his venison cooking – did he hang it for three weeks? 'Now't o' t' sort,' he said. 'Tell your missus it wants cooking slow, an' basting well wi' plenty o' bacon fat. Take a five-mile walk before breakfast and you'll wish you'd bought a haunch.'

And your chefs may say what they like, we cooked ours as he advised and it was delicious. And I'm wishing I *could* take a five-mile tramp over the moors before breakfast – and I certainly ought to have bought a haunch.

The signpost in Rievaulx village.

Changes on the Moor

Photographs of Jim Dale (with thigh length overtrousers) and other workers
on the Duncombe Park Estate with a captured deer (above) and (below) with transport.
Note the high wooden fence to prevent deer jumping out of the enclosed park.
(From photographs loaned by Peter Braithwaite.)

The last time I dropped in to see Jim Dale was during the war. I found him leaning against a larch tree, mopping his brow and fanning himself gently with his weathered tweed hat. Brown as a berry, slim and agile, he had just finished a ten-mile jaunt over the wildest part of North Yorkshire. 'Ten mile is a'most as much as I can manage nowadays,' he told me ruefully. 'What wi' me rifle and ammunition and field glasses. Makes me sweat a bit on a yat day like this.'

It certainly made me sweat, and I had tramped a mere four miles and I'm thirty years younger than Jim. Never before had I heard him admit being tired. It seemed incredible. As we walked towards his stone house on the hillside he showed no sign of it and I guessed that he was down in the mouth over something. Perhaps there was some truth in the rumour I had heard in Helmsley. Was he really going to retire? If so I could realise the cause of his obvious despondency; he would simply hate the idea of leaving the moor.

His only absence from this lovely spot was during the First World War when he went with Lord Feversham and the Yeoman Rifles to France. He was, I had been told, a very effective sniper. I could never persuade him to talk about the war but he did say often how much he hated being away from his own corner of Yorkshire. A new officer, a Devon man, and therefore a 'foreigner' in Jim's estimation, once said to him. 'Dale! For Pete's sake speak slower, man, and speak proper grammar and use a few words of English. I can't make out what you're blabbering about!' Jim was furious. This was more than he could stand; Yorkshire was being insulted. 'Ah dean't know hoo ya dare stand theer, sorr, an' say sike a thing! Allow me sorr, ti tell ya summat: if there is ya spot iv all England wheer foalks speak pure English – Ah said PURE ENGLISH, SORR – it's up in that lahtle spot i' Yorkshire wheer ah cum fra!' To him 'England' meant Ryedale and its capital was Helmsley town.

As we walked along I naturally enquired after the deer. Jim stopped and looked at me severely. 'Ain't you heard? There's nobbut a few outliggers left. Aye, we've a'most polished 'em all off. The herd's finished aboot, like me. We had a desperate do a-killin' 'em. All sort o' toffs I had, shooting along wi' me, Scot's Guards an' Irish Guards and Coldstream Guards and Grenadiers – an' some on 'em couldn't shoot for toffee! I've happen taught some of 'em a thing or two for when they went ower the watter.' Conditions on Scawton Moor had made it imperative to kill the whole herd of some two hundred and fifty reds. Fences and walls were broken down, for during the past year his moorland had echoed with a thousand alien noises and great monsters of steel dashed up hill and down dale belching fire and smoke. They had smashed through thickets, toppled down stone walls and swept over the boundary fences. The Tank Corps were rehearsing for their coming battles and when they eventually clattered through the apple orchards of Normandy they bore on their sides the emblem, *The Men of the Moors.* I wondered how the deer had reacted to this disturbance, Jim told me, 'Oh, some of 'em seemed to enjoy it! I've seen some hinds trotting alongside them tanks, interested like. Happen they thought it was a new sort o' stag.' It was impossible to keep the walls and fences in repair. 'There's not a dog-waller left in this whole countryside,' said Jim, 'an' if there was one he'd have ower mich work on somewhere else. Of course t' deer got oot, so we've had to sacrifice the herd. Wars is no good to nobody.'

We came to his stone-built house, where I enjoyed a real Yorkshire tea. We had just finished when down came the rain in buckets-full, a proper deluge that meant a sodden road for my homeward tramp. No car can get within miles of his home and it's rough going for a horse and trap. 'I'll see you safe across the valley,' said Jim, and he harnessed up the galloway. In places the road was so steep that we had to walk and Jim led the pony. When we forded the Rye the water came up to the floorboards. 'You should be here in winter, mun. Sometimes we're cut off for weeks what wi' snow and flood. My hoosekeeper was a-sitting perched up on top of this trap ti keep her feet dry when one wheel dropped into a hole and she tippled off, end-ower-end like. All I could see was summat round bulging up out o' t' watter, but I managed to grab it just in time and I turned her right road up and hauled her aboard. She were a'most dead, nearly frozen, so I got turned round and home as fast as t'owd pony could leg it, and I roasted her out again in front of the great fire and got some brandy into her and she were not a penny the wuss. My word, I was reet scared – housekeepers is difficult to find in this quarter.'

He wondered what would happen to his grand home.

'Nobody would stick it in winter,' said Jim. 'Why, snow piles up high and you can't get out for days. Talk about the wilds o' Canada. They can't hev nowt to touch it!' When he had got rid of the two or three 'outliggers' – all that remained of the famous herd – Jim himself would become an outligger too. He had a tidy little place to go to in the market town, but he was a bit doubtful about it. 'There'll be no view worth owt – only walls and sich like. Mun, you should see yon wood in autumn, all glowin' wi' every shade o' colour ever created. And you should sniff this air of a morning early – it's marvellous! But there is one consolation, I'll have somebody to talk to down there.'

After leaving Jim I joined the postman who didn't sound very enthusiastic about the keeper of the deer. 'For many a bright year,' he told me, 'we used to put his letters in a box on t'edge oft' park over there. But one neet t' Postmaster General were talkin' on t' wireless about how everybody got their mail delivered at least so many times a week. Old Jim were listening in and he collars pen and paper and he writes him a letter – tells him straight he were talking rot! Couple o' days later up come a fellow fra' Lundon, one of them lah-di-dah chaps, makes me walk along with him, measures t' mileage and clocks the time. Next thing we got told to take Mr. James Dale's mail to his residence. Eeh, but I did cus! Still, never mind, I thought, it mebbe won't happen more than once a month, cause he didn't have such a lot o' letters, like. But I calculated without Old Jim – he fair capped me, did Jim. He goes and orders a daily paper to be posted to him, and I hev it ti take, rain or shine. Now *I'll* be thunderin' glad when he *does* retire.'

I turned for one last look at Jim's pony and cart, crawling like an ant up the distant moorland slope. So long, Jim. You've certainly loved life on the moors; you've gladdened the hearts of thousands with your rustic wit and laughter in the market place. You've earned the right to a change, to sit in the sun and spin yarns in the company of your cronies. But when that old rifle of yours cracks for the last time, Jim, and the last lone stag drops on the heather I know it'll seem tough. You've certainly loved those tall deer.

Jim Dale (third from left) and Duncombe Park workers with captured deer.
(From a photograph loaned by Peter Braithwaite.)

The Outligger's Return

Jim Dale had never relished the idea of retirement. 'There'll be nowt doon there worth seein', nobbut bricks and mortar,' he said. Of course I knew exactly what he meant: that the moor had been his domain for fifty years and leaving his home at Antofts was going to hurt him. He was certainly not despising the attractions of the trim little town of Helmsley where he had lingered each market day till 'tonnin' oot tahme'. Losing the deer and leaving Scawton Moor worried the old man much more than his cronies in Helmsley ever realised. Jim laughed and joked about 'flitting', but it was obvious to me that he had little heart for his new life. Unhappily he did not long survive the change.

A year or two passed by before I walked across that moor again, headed for Antofts. 'It's none such a bad lahtle spot to live at when all's said and done,' Jim used to say, which was his way of telling me how much he loved his home. He went there as a young man with his bride and they were happy there together. He lost her some years before the war. That old house meant a great deal to Jim. As I tramped through the heather my mind was filled with pleasant memories. Over there by that group of furze was the deep gully where we had watched two great stags fighting for nearly an hour; it was in that patch of bracken where I found a fawn – the first I had ever seen – and it took my heart by storm; down by the river, just round that bend, we came across the two stags locked together by their antlers and Jim had sent me back to the homestead to fetch a saw and a rope. What a job that was, getting the pair free! Happy and exciting days, now, alas, long ago.

The moor seemed to have changed. It was strangely quiet and deserted. Then on a distant slope I spotted a herd of black Galloway bullocks. A few minutes later I found myself before a great stretch of newly-sown grassland, fifty acres or more, with a hundred cross-bred Leicester ewes contentedly grazing on it. What a transformation! I never expected cattle or sheep up here on Scawton Moor. Further on I came to fields of barley and oats, and very good crops they were too. Why, there were six or seven hundred acres of reclaimed land. It was almost unbelievable.

As I drew nearer to Jim's old home I began to wonder what sort of folks had taken it over. Perhaps they wouldn't want a trespasser nosing round. I was uncertain whether to go on or not but my curiosity decided me to have a last look round the old place. Soon I caught sight of it nestling among the pines and larches, but it looked odd somehow, with no smoke rising from the chimney. I heard no dog barking. As I came closer there seemed to be not the slightest sign of life about the house. Surely somebody must live there? The wind whistled dolefully through the pines, and old buildings were empty and forlorn. The stable door lay flat and the yard gates were broken. The whole place was a shambles. Nearing the house I saw broken windows. There was a wide gap in the roof and broken tiles littered the pathway to the door that swung to and fro in the wind. In the garden nettles and rose bay willow herb were in firm possession.

I turned away. I simply could not bring myself to look inside the rooms where so often I had been Jim's welcome guest, so I wandered back to the buildings, to the butcher's shop, to the cowhouse, the barn, the stable. Loose on the fallen stable door was a horse shoe, one off Jim's 'owd Gallowa', a smallish shoe which he had nailed there for luck. I knew it well enough, for I had been with him when he put it there many years ago. I wrenched it off and slipped it in my pocket, just for luck. We dalesmen may pretend we don't believe in these absurd superstitions but deep in our hearts we're not so very sure. 'I'll polish it and hang it up in my room, not for luck of course – that's silly – but as a souvenir of Antofts.' And at this very moment as I write it hangs on the wall above my desk.

The pony shoe from Antofts now hangs over my desk as I edit these stories.

Turning my back on the deserted house I strode quickly away, a lump in my throat, over the heather. My short cut brought me close to the edge of a ravine and I looked down among the trees. It was growing dusk but I fancied I saw something down there, probably more black cattle, I thought. There was a good deal of brushwood in the way; I could see nothing distinctly. I shall never quite understand why I should keep on peering down that gully or why I suddenly rushed to a place where I could get a clearer view. I ran some fifty yards, then I saw them! Cattle, my foot! These were deer! Yes, deer! Thirty or forty of 'em! There was a sudden flurry amid the bushes below in the valley and a stag stepped out beside the beck. I waited motionless while he stood there sniffing the breeze. Then the scent of man reached him and he sprang aside with a great bound! The little herd vanished and all I could see was the crinkled line of brushwood. As I walked away I could scarcely believe that I had really seen them. Perhaps my imagination had played me some strange trick. In any case it was almost dark and my eyes are not what they used to be . . .

It was quite dark when I reached civilisation. 'Deer?' said the man in the pub. 'Aye, there's happen forty deer on Scawton Moor. A few must ha' got away when they had that big shootin' do a few years back. Red un's? I dunno for certain aboot it, but they do say as quite a few are knocking aboot in them woods belongin' Forestry Commission by Ampleforth. A chap told me t'other day that they'd shot a reight big stag there last week – must ha' been the daddy of 'em all, for he weighed round twenty-fahve stone.' The landlord joined in. 'You seem interested in deer. Did you ever happen across Old Jim Dale any time? He knew a bit aboot deer.'

I nodded and bade them goodnight as I fingered the horseshoe in my pocket. Then I drove away, fifty miles away, for I was what Jim used to call an 'outligger', meaning one that had got away to a pasture elsewhere.

I was with Stephen in 1956 when we tramped across the moor to Antofts and he found the pony shoe. A quarter of a century later this walk was to be recalled as I overheard, in a conversation of a teaching colleague, Peter Braithwaite, the name 'Jim Dale'. I asked if this was 'gamekeeper Jim' and received a look of astonishment. Jim was Peter's relative and had been tracked down as part of a family history study. Later, to my delight, Peter produced his family photographs of Jim himself with the deer.

Antofts in 1986 now immaculately restored to life. I wonder if the children who play on the swing which hangs from the tree just outside the dry stone wall ever see any of the descendants of Jim's outligger deer?

I went to Scawton recently one frosty November day when the air was clear and the bracken appeared orange against the first winter snow. White woodsmoke columns rising straight up identified the positions of each moorland home. I called down to one farmer's wife hanging out the washing, from a path rising steeply above her buildings. The side of the farmhouse was piled high with logs to last through the winter. She was suspicious of me until I mentioned Jim Dale. Her face cleared: 'Yes . . . that's the path to Antofts . . . I had Jim's niece staying with me recently . . . Up there . . .'

Beyond Scawton Moor the guns banged and in one clearing off the main road an untidy litter of muddy Range Rovers and Shoguns waited for the 'shots' to return. I remember sitting with my wife in the front window of the Black Swan, *eating delicious scones laden with jam and cream, when one such posse of vehicles arrived and disgorged its loads of gentlemen 'shots' who trailed through the hotel in a cloud of good-quality tweed with rather dirty, tired dogs at heel. The beaters and guides carried sticks over their shoulders heavy with game. Jim would have approved.*

Captured by the French

Near the end of the war our road was captured by the French – lock, stock and barrel. They came, saw and conquered us one hot afternoon in May. One minute I was engrossed in writing, the next minute there they were, right in front of my window, a little group of tired-looking, dusty lads in khaki, chattering French. Across the road they had lined up their vehicles with unfamiliar markings, tricolour pennons and the red cross of Lorraine, a colourful convoy.

I popped into the garden to get a better view, then something amazing happened. It was just as though some radio instruction had gone to each housewife in our street, for out they all came carrying trays of tea – best china services at that. I saw Mrs. Bramble had even her solid silver tray out, the one old Bramble got when he retired. Staid and dignified matrons vied with each other in the elegance of their smiling hospitality. All along the street were Frenchmen, bowing, saluting, smiling, pressing packets of chocolate and tins of food on the children. 'Souvenir, *très bon chocolat*', they said. I spotted young Jackie Morris doing well, with his pockets full and running home with an armful of tins. At my gate five French lads were gathered round little Janet, a flaxen-haired ten-year-old, offering sweets and marvelling at her colouring, her plumpness, her English beauty. Others, with a wealth of gesture, were trying to answer schoolgirls frantically whipping over the pages of their dictionaries. In less than half an hour all the world seemed to have gathered, children swarming over lorries and tanks, old and young giving out invitations right and left. It was all rather undignified, decidedly un-English, but if ever there was an *Entente Cordiale,* well, this was it!

That same evening three young fellows in their early twenties, spick and span, stood on my doorstep, clicked their heels and saluted. My wife beamed and said how delighted she was that they had remembered to come, ordered me to stand by to entertain and explained, *'Monsieur parle français très bien'*. She had been doing her homework to learn that much. Poor *'monsieur'* hadn't spoken French since 1919 but we got along quite nicely. In fact I was complimented on my excellent accent and felt rather pleased with myself. The three were delightful lads, very diplomatic, well-mannered. Jean was a farmer's son from near Marseilles, very dark, almost Italian; Louis was a baker from Avignon and Georges a blond miner from Dijon. I called them the *Three Musketeers* and they laughed politely. None of them knew much English except 'Tank you ver' much' and 'Beer très good' and 'Pretty Miss'. None had seen or heard from his family for three years or more; none had seen inside an English home before. They were frankly amazed to find we were not starving, that we were so well equipped, that everybody in England was making 'total war', that we had land girls and women porters and so on.

When my daughter came home they bowed to her and Jean ceremoniously offered a chair. When my wife made for the door Georges was off the mark in a flash to open it for her. When she brought in the food Louis paid handsome compliments to her baking and pastry making. Within a few minutes they certainly captured the hearts of my womenfolk. It had delighted them much, they said, to receive so warm a welcome; they had never dreamed of being received into the house of an English gentleman and his lady. I blushed. We were all so kind and was it not a happy chance to meet a *monsieur* who spoke such excellent, such really perfect French? Was not his voice so clear and agreeable? It wasn't long before I too liked the lads immensely. They even laughed at my jokes. 'Come again tomorrow', I said.

Next day I took them round the garden where they went into raptures over the flowers like the ones they had at home – gilly flowers, forget-me-nots, irises for instance. Our trees and flowering shrubs our hedgerows and green fields were all so sweet and fresh after the heat and dust of the Africa they had recently left. 'And what weather! So much pleasanter even than the Riviera,' said Jean. He soon became disillusioned on that point, of course, but that first week was ideal. He declared that England was so beautiful that he would even love to stay here after the war and work on a farm. He could work hard and perhaps he might marry some fair English girl. Never in his life had he seen complexions so perfect as those of the beautiful land girls . . . The baker lad wanted to get back to France, that was all. He was happy to think that his family would still have plenty to eat since they were bakers and could not be really rationed. That thought was ever with him. He much admired this England but France was his land and there was a girl at home he was some day to marry.

They impressed us very favourably and we learned a lot from each other. We met several other lads also – Marcel, who played the accordion beautifully, Maurice, a student who wished to become a journalist and who had read French translations of Kipling – *Kim, Puck o' Pook's Hill, Stalky* – and we talked on literature for hours. Their captain, a man of about my own age, had his son with him, a very young lieutenant. I remember the captain saying, 'Even when France fell I did not doubt, never. I took my son, my two daughters and my wife, and we got away. This day I am posted as a rebel in my own town. A traitor now has possession of my house, my offices, all my belongings. When I return I shall meet him and he shall repay.' He loved to listen to my daughter's schoolgirl French and rejoiced that she did not smoke. Neither did his daughters. I think he enjoyed most of all to see my flaxen-haired five-year-old, fresh from his bath, being tucked into bed. 'These are the things that matter,' he said. 'These are the things we are fighting for. So we shall win the victory for our sons and daughters that we love.'

We knew them only a few days, then they rode away to join the final assault on the enemy. A happy lot they were too as they waved us goodbye. They were making for home.

Ploughing – with Horses

I love towns so little that I never go to them unless my journey is really necessary. But one day last month when an all-conquering sun had swept from our little Wolds village the last veils of morning mist I set off for the metropolis, Hull. I took my reluctant roundabout way through pleasant country lanes to the village of Skidby, and in the clear air of morning the windmill on the hill stood out jet-black and gleaming white. I was in the mood to welcome a chance to stop and stare and I found myself reciting some lines I learned as a lad:

'It grinds the corn for man and beast
That all of 'em can have a feast,
The motion of our mill is swift
And t'miller has to practise thrift
And jump around to get things done
Or else his mill will cease to run.'

Skidby Mill. Built in 1821 and owned by the East Yorkshire Borough of Beverley. It is the only working mill north of the Humber. Now restored it is a museum of agriculture and milling. Visitors can buy genuine stone-ground flour.

At Skidby the modern miller still jumps around to get things done –

assisted by electricity. The sails no longer turn the millstones, he has the very latest machinery inside, all electric. But blessings upon him for preserving for us who pass by one of the finest landmarks of the country.

If mechanisation has claimed the mill it has not succeeded in banishing the horse from Skidby's farms. Alas, there is not one single horse of any description left in my village, so I rejoiced exceedingly at the sight of a fine grey mare drawing a cart down Skidby Hill. Then I discovered the farmer swinging a scythe and for half an hour we talked farming. Yes, he still stuck to his horses, just because he liked 'em. He always had liked horses, and his favourites had always been greys; he still had three of 'em. That 'en in the cart there was Lorna, and Bonnie and Bessie were ploughin', just over t'rise back there. So off I went to look at them. Hull could wait.

Hundreds of seagulls wheeled around, following closely as the plough slid towards me, harness making music as the big greys wheeled along the headland with the mouldboard flashing silver in their wake. Without even a glance in my direction the ploughman completed the half-circle and sank the plough into the soil again, then, 'Whoa!' The horses turned enquiring heads in my direction while their master fished in his pocket.

'Have a fag?' I said.

He thanked me and we smoked, taking stock of each other, saying nothing much but thinking a lot – country fashion.

'Nice pair.'

'Aye, not so bad. Bit o' blood in Betty though, rather mettlesome first thing of a mornin' sometimes.'

Of *course* he liked horses best! He had been a market gardener, but gave it up a few years back. Why? A fiddlin' job it was, not to be compared with working wi' hosses.

'Handy little plough this. Made in Driffield?' and I stepped down into the furrow, grasped the handles and the plough strings. Then it happened. The greys leaned forward, the plough slid gently through the soil and we were off. This was more than I'd bargained for.

The ploughman smiled. 'Keep 'er goin,' he said, so I pulled myself together, tightened my grip and felt for the balance. As we forged ahead the plough heaved and swayed over folds and ridges with me leaning this way and that like a sailor on the sea. Before long I realised with a great joy that I had found the knack of it and I fell into the measured stride that matched the rhythm of the team. My journey, my car, my job no longer existed; I was once more a leggy lad of twelve, with cord breeches and hob-nailed boots, peering forward, intent only on a straight furrow. We plodded on. It seemed an immeasurable distance to the hedge. Chains were a-jingling, one wheel discordantly squeaking, seagulls plaintively calling. My back ached; perspiration trickled down my face; I puffed like a grampus as we neared the headland. Now for it! The greys stepped out more briskly as we swung into the turn. Instinctively I handled the plough strings and leaned sideways on the handles as we swayed round by the hedge in the smoothest of curves and into the furrow again. Sweating at every pore, breathless with excitement, I stumbled into position, and never, never have I felt so pleased as when, at exactly the right moment, I jerked my hands upward and the share dived into the soil again, clean as a whistle.

'Whoa!' I panted, and we stopped. I took out a cigarette and walked across to look at my work – and to recover my poise. Yes . . . it seemed a pretty decent bit of work, straight as a die, or at any rate I thought so. 'Um, not half bad,' said the ploughman. 'It never leaves ye. Aye, you've still got it.' I threw out my chest a bit, for after all it's no mean achievement to be able to plough a straight furrow. It was a really jolly old world that sunny morning. It was good to be alive.

When I reached Hull one of my friends looked at my shoes. 'Where on earth have you been?'

'Ploughing,' I answered, casual like, 'with hosses.'

It was the first time in forty-eight years.

The young Stephen would have seen this team of working horses when staying with his Aunt at Harome.
(Rye House Farm in 1906. Photograph loaned by Enid and John Bulmer.)

Shepherd of the Wolds

From time immemorial the high Wolds have been grazed by sheep. Stone Age men who dug the many dikes and entrenchments near Huggate would watch their flocks of puny little animals up there on the wind-swept hills. Today the East Riding farmers keep some four hundred thousand of the finest sheep in Britain, not on natural pastures but folded on turnips or kale or clover, to tread firm the thin chalky soil, to manure it and make it fit for corn again. Farming on the Wolds means mostly corn – and sheep. When men congregate the talk is invariably of ewes and lambs, gimmers, tegs, hogs, shearlings, weathers and tups. When they disagree it is usually about the superiority of Leicesters or Border Leicesters or Suffolks.

One winter we talked for some weeks about a flock of sheep that had strayed from the fold. My farmer friend, Amos Hoggard, took a casual look at his flock in the turnip field one morning, then counted them. There were eighty too many. Mind you, they do get a few wanderers occasionally, but eighty was almost another flock. As he said, 'They were makin' a bit of a 'ole in me tonnups,' so he rang up all his neighbours and the local shepherds, checked and re-checked, but nobody for miles around had lost even one ewe lamb. Finally, after a few days, he notified the police but they too sought in vain for the owner of the eighty strays. One week passed – two weeks – three weeks, and still the eighty were not claimed and remained devouring his turnips. The whole countryside was agog; the mystery was discussed in every market place and in every pub; at long last, at a farm a few miles away, a flock was found to be eighty short. In the *Wolds Inn* where shepherds congregate it was the sensation of a lifetime. 'Sike a goin' on 'ad nivver 'appened roond 'ere in t'memory o'man.'

A shepherd as a rule is a man of few words. He weighs each word carefully, speaks slowly and quietly and there is about him an air of security and gentleness, acquired no doubt through solitary work among ewes and lambs. Such a man had a hut on the skyline and, as it was a sunny afternoon after a cold, frosty morning, I walked across the field for a chat. The soil clung to my boots in cumbersome clods but the air was crystal clear and I could see afar off the towers of Beverley Minster, the silver streak of the Humber and the cooling tower at Hull, fully twenty-five miles away. The shepherd and his dog met me at the hut. 'Grand day,' I said. He shook his head. 'Nay, not for sheep.' I waited awhile. 'Rather have snow and frost. Enough snow to cover turnips, frost to mak' ground dry an' easy to walk on. Today it's all wet and blathery – theer coats gets all clotted up wi' soil, like your boots. They come a deal healthier at lambin' time wi' snow and frost.'

There were some six hundred sheep in the fold, two hundred of them Leicesters and the rest Leicester-Suffolk crosses. The Leicester flock had been here for seventy years and he had been their shepherd for fifty. 'Leicesters stand t'weather on t'Wolds better than any. It's cold up 'ere in winter. Long wool they have – it keeps 'em warm.' I know well how the east winds sweep unfettered from the sea to cut more cruelly than anywhere in England. I have seen the snow pile up in gigantic drifts to isolate villages for a week.

'How did you manage in the winter of '47?'

'Oh, that were a wonderful lambin' time! Mind you, for weeks they didn't get more'n half a tonnup apiece a day so we had to feed hand meat. I remember one Sunday morning when I went down to t'eighty-acre, where we'd twelve hundred sheep I couldn't see above a hundred.'

'Buried?'

'Aye, they were an' all! Six of us, poking down wi' hedge stakes were at it from eight o'clock till fower findin' 'em. We had t'dogs to help, of course; never ha' managed without 'em. Onnyroad, we got 'em all out and none of 'em was any worse.'

With him it wasn't just a job from 7.30 to 5; it was his hobby and time was never considered. It wasn't easy, he told me, to get young chaps to tackle a shepherd's job nowadays, though some farm students would if they were keen to get on. There's a lot to learn and it was really a scientific job, especially breeding. 'We keep detailed records for every yow,' he said. 'Then there's shows and what's more excitin' than a big show? It tak's a lot of science an' good management to produce winners. First there's mating, to get just the proper sort, an' then there's feeding. No shepherd can turn out champions unless the boss buys the best possible grub for 'em.'

I asked him what were the hall-marks of a prize-winning ram, but he was a little cagey in his reply.

'First, a good head on 'im. Then he wants a good straight back. Next he mun have fower good legs, yan at each corner!'

'Then what about the preparation for judging?'

'Oh, that? I just trim 'im up a bit, mak 'im look nice. Come now you don't expect me to tell you all my little secrets, do you?' He was too modest to tell me exactly how many prizes his charges had won; he had probably lost count a few years earlier. He did admit that they had won not only 'Firsts' but 'Championships' for four years running at the Royal, for three years running at the Great Yorkshire, and the Longwool Championship at Smithfield for two successive years. He couldn't remember mere 'prizes'. As shepherd he had been awarded 'a fair number o' silver mugs o' wun sort and another'. Each year he meets all England's leading shepherds at the principal shows and sales. They sometimes live together for as long as eight or ten days and they talk of little else but sheep, and the verdict of the judges, of course.

'Funny thing is,'he said, 'none of 'em except me seem to agree wi' t'judges.' I said that there would be many shepherds who dealt with other breeds than Leicesters. 'Of course, but I nobbut mix up wi' Leicester shepherds. Us Leicester men don't reckon to bother much wi' Suffolk chaps, let alone them others. Mind you, fettling up a Suffolk for a show is nobbut an armchair sort o' job! Compared wi' a Leicester tup weighing aboot twenty-four stone, a Suffolk is just a lamb.'

He told me of three pedigree rams being shipped abroad to several countries, and chuckled, 'We sent some to owd Nasser in Egypt. He's going to cross his sheep wi' Leicesters and feed 'em on lucerne. Looks as though he's going to have some proper sheep is owd Nasser.'

He was awarded the B.E.M. 'for services to agriculture' and was asked to appear on B.B.C. television. I was not surprised when he declined. 'T.V's nowt i' my line,' he assured me, 'so I told 'em I was ower throng. Besides, they wanted me to go on a Friday, an' that happened to be t'day I'd arranged to go to Driffield for a haircut.'

A few weeks later Ernest Boddy, the shepherd, went for a day or two to Scarborough and was killed crossing the road. The funeral service was attended by farmers from all over England. The tributes paid to this grand countryman by the local shepherds can be summed up in the words spoken by one of them: 'He were a gentleman and the champion shepherd of England.'

Farewell to Fred

When Maggie Oldcastle came round to tell us that Fred Stockton was leaving the village it really shook us. We're only a small community, not more than 150 all told, and Fred's departure would leave a tremendous gap. He was bred and born at South End, farmed five hundred acres, was Chairman of the Parish Council and Treasurer for the church. 'Aye, he's selling up, bought a bungalow at seaside, retiring for good,' said Maggie, 'but we can't let him go without a present, so I'm collectin'. Nobody has to put down more'n half-a-crown,' and she took out her notebook. South End Farm was knocked down for £8000 and Fred's stock and implements made a few more thousands, then Fred was ready for off.

The last Sunday evening he was with us saw the church crowded out, not an empty seat anywhere. In fact they fetched some forms from the school to accommodate those who had to squeeze in at the back. Everybody who wasn't bed-ridden had turned out, even the chapel folk. Some were there who hadn't looked inside a church since they were wed. There was nothing very special about the service and the sermon was no different from usual, but the singing was just wonderful. Some of us wondered if the roof would stand it. Then at the finish the choir walked out, but everybody else sat still and waited.

There wasn't a sound, not a whisper, when Maggie Oldcastle stood up in her pew and rustled up the aisle to the chancel steps. 'We all know why we're stoppin' behind a bit,' she said, and placed a little parcel on the lectern. 'We all know Fred Stockton's off to leave us. I've known him sixty year and I've always called him Fred an' I can't change now. So, Fred, we've all clubbed together to buy you a little present, an' there it is. You'll ha' to come oot and get it.'

The old farmer half rose in his pew and shook his head. 'Nay, nay, Maggie, you nivver owt to ha' done it! You shouldn't ha' done it! You nivver owt to hev.'

'Why, we hev done it,' she answered briskly, and held up the parcel, 'so come on wi' ye.'

Fred walked slowly up the church, shaking his head. 'Ah didn't want owt like this. Ah've done nowt ti disarve it.' Then he stood beside Maggie to face the crowded congregation. She handed him the parcel, with, 'There it is, Fred. And this little book has al' t'names of your friends in. You can look at your present if you like.' He looked thoughtfully at the parcel and weighed it on the palm of his hand. 'I'm wonderin' what can be inside it? Nowt very big, it's nobbut leet. I'm hoping . . . mebbe it's a watch. D'ye know, I've saved up time and time again to buy a watch but ivery time summat else was wanted for t'farm and I never managed to buy one. Now this looks as if it might be a watch, and it feels like a watch.' Then he slowly opened the parcel. His face lit up, delighted, and he held up his hand. 'By gum, it is a watch!' he cried.

Then the vicar said a few words and the churchwardens said their pieces, after which Maggie strapped the watch on Fred's wrist. 'It's been kind of you all,' he said, 'and I'm no talker, I hardly know how to thank you. You couldn't have given me owt nicer. Now, I'm going to stand at door there and catch each one of you as you go oot.' As his neighbours filed solemnly past, each nodded and shook his hand. So, at our ancient parish church we said farewell to Fred.

From his seaside residence he goes each week to our market town to join a group of his old friends at the cattle market. Someone is sure to say, 'My word, its gettin' latish on. I'll have to be off home. Who's gotten reight time?' All eyes turned to Fred last week. He shot out his left hand, pulled back his cuff and announced, 'Accordin' to Greenwich it's just twenty-fower minutes past two,' pleased as a dog with two tails.

Farndale – Flocks and Fellowship

At ten o'clock one Saturday morning I left East Moors, tramped along to Bransdale and rejoiced to find it had not changed in the slightest since I was a boy. I doubt if it has changed much since Brand, the Saxon, rode this way. The little Hodge Beck still burbles past the mill, but alas! there is no village, no shop, no inn, nor have I any relative there, so I climbed the steep eastward slope and soon crossed Rudland Rigg, the road that runs along the ridge, 1200 feet high. From where I stood leaning against a stone wall I could view the valley of Farndale, the whole beauteous length of it, seven miles spread below me like a map.

I had been standing there only a few minutes when I met the first human being in six long miles of tramping, a young farmer whose motor-bike and side-car were down the lane. He came straight to me.

'Excuse me. Ah seed you comin' ower t'moor a while back, you were steppin' oot as brisk as bottled yal *(ale)* and Ah thowt you looked like sorta chap as wouldn't miss owt much. Did you happen across twelve ewes marked red rudd on near shou'der?'

'Sorry,' I said. 'Ah've seen some o' Watsons, some o' Fothergills and a few o' Garbett's, but Ah've seen nowt o' yours.'

He 'gawped' a moment at that, then asked, 'D'ye belong roond here then?' It seemed that he had bought forty ewes from a farmer at the top end of Farndale, but, as he said, 't'owd drover chap nobbut 'livered twenty-eight at station. Bit weak in t'head he is, but he thinks he must ha' lost 'em somewhere aboot 'ere.'

It was my turn to ask where he came from. He named a village near York.

'Down in the low country,' I remarked, for no special reason except that we men from the moors have a certain pity for those unfortunates from the flatter districts. 'You chaps from t'low country usually know nowt aboot moor sheep.' He was indignant, told me he had bought lots in his time; there wasn't much he didn't know about sheep. I teased him a little. 'Thoo doesn't seem to know t'first thing aboot moor yows that's lost.'

'An what might that be?' he asked.

'They're like homin' pigeons – they make for home. All you have to do is to get away to the man you bought 'em off. They'll be home by this time!'

He was a little dubious, but finally he thanked me kindly, said he'd go to the farm at Dale End, and turned on his heel. I called out, 'If you like, I'll come with you.' The truth is that I was sick of walking. He seemed pleased to have me as a passenger. The side-car was very obviously a farmer's. It had been used to transport sheep, poultry and artificial manures, and I eyed it with some misgiving. My friend improved matters somewhat by means of a few handfuls of bracken; then I wedged myself into the boat-shaped box and away we went. I have, of course, visited Hull Fair as well as Blackpool and I have experienced their switch backs and the big wheels; but they are as nothing compared with the thrills of riding in a sidecar over those particular moorland roads. Finally we lurched to a full stop.

'We're 'ere!' said the driver, pointing. Down below us I saw the stone house and farmstead. I could almost look down the chimney.

'How on earth do you get to it?' I asked.

'Doon this 'ere cart track,' he said. It was a perilous-looking slope.

'Ah'll git oot,' I decided, lapsing into dialect again, then I slithered down a steep track till I reached the stackyard gate, which in my earlier years was the 'staggarth yat'. Beyond it I saw three children playing, sliding off a stack down to a heap of loose straw. The eldest boy would be about ten and I hailed them. 'Hi there! Is your father in?' They stood for a few seconds, looking me over. Then with one accord they shot off like frightened rabbits into the house, and the cry went up, 'Mam! There's a man!'

Into the doorway there came a stout matronly figure wearing a coarse apron, her arms and hands covered in flour. The children peeped shyly from behind her voluminous skirts.

'It's all right, missus, I'm with the man who bought them forty sheep – he's lost a dozen somewhere. There he is, coming in staggarth yat.'

'I'm sorry the maister isn't in,' she said 'He's leading a lahtle jag *(small load)* o' hay to some beasts in t'valley field, but I'll send bairns for him – he won't be long. You'd better come in and sit a bit. Would you like a bit o' summat to eat?'

I admitted that I should appreciate it, so she fetched one of those big, round cottage loaves, held it against her bib and sawed off a slice after plastering it liberally with butter, the salty butter, freshly made, that I greatly love. Next she covered the slice with ham, placed a second buttered slice on top, cut it into four great sandwiches and passed it to me. It completely covered a large dinner plate. The young farmer sat beside me on the settle and I held the plate towards him, but our hostess cried, 'No, no! That's for you. I'll cut him one for hisself. We'd better have a cup o' tea as well,' and she went out into the yard. I heard the pump rattling, clankety-clank, and then she came in with one of the biggest kettles I have ever seen. My companion murmured behind his hand,

'That'll nivver boil i' six months,' but the poor low-country fellow knew nothing of the power of turf fires. It was not long before tea was made, just as the master came in.

'Lost twelve o' them ewes, the bairn tells me. That's a bad job.'

'Aye, it's varry bad,' my companion agreed, 'I mun ha' them twelve back soon, them yows is all t'brass I hev, and next month I'm aimin' to git wed.'

That statement certainly roused our hostess. 'Eeh – fancy that,' she breathed; then she asked, 'Is she anybody I know?' The prospective bridegroom spoke of his fiancee with enthusiasm, and our hostess said, 'I think I know 'er – seen 'er in Kirbymoorside market with two sisters. That's right! I know which one – she certainly *is* a bonny gel.'

Her husband chimed in: 'Main thing has nowt to do with havin' a pretty face! Me fayther always tell'd me to have a good look at 'er 'ands! What sort of a worker is she? That's the main point.' The young man said he felt sure he was getting a good worker, then the older man continued his advice. 'Mind you get a good-natured 'un. Hev nowt to do with them that natter an' jabber an' gan on with the "nivver-give-ower". And may the Lord deliver you from one o' them hoose-proud women that mak' you leave yer boots ootside. Me fayther always tell'd me "There's no happiness in a hoose when t'kettle's bright all ower."' I glanced at his cheerful wife and the big black kettle and applauded his father's wisdom.

'That's all very well,' said the young man, 'but what's the chances of my twelve yows coming back 'ere?'

'Oh, they'll come back all right,' the farmer assured him. 'They always do. Mind you Ah won't guarantee they'll return straight away, but they certainly will. Maybe next year. Sometimes they get away to t'other side o' t'river and then they eat their way nice and steady round by Roseberry Topping and then come back, happen two year after. Mind you, when they're away that long they usually bring a nice little family with 'em.'

The young lover almost wailed, 'I can't wait that long! I want 'em back sharp, or I'll be short o' brass.' The older man grinned, patted him on the shoulder and promised 'Me and me dogs'll find 'em for you tomorrow morn. They'll not be far off,' at which the low-country man left for home, greatly comforted.

The farmer turned to me with a smile: 'I like the look o' you. Come wi' me an' I'll show you my missus's front garden,' and he led the way down a passage, opened the little-used front door with some difficulty and stood on the doorstep. I looked round in vain for the front garden.

He grinned, then swept his arms round to point to the dale: 'There's her garden, mister, all Farndale! Twenty thousand acres of the bonniest bit of Britain. I've had men up 'ere in war time, Americans, Canadians, Scotsmen and Irishmen, all sorts and sizes and colours, and they all say this is as pretty a spot as owt they've ever seen.' I agreed with him enthusiastically. Farndale will take some beating. Then he went on, 'You must come again to see us. Come in harvest time, when valley's filled wi' corn and heather's all in bloom on the hills! Come in spring time and see daffodils – acres and acres of 'em in the valley growing wild. Come onnytime! She's always worth lookin' at.'

I said I might stay around for a day or two if there was room in the inn, whereupon he left me suddenly and I heard him call, 'Missus! Get best bed ready. He's stoppin' wi' us.' That night I slept on the deepest and softest of feather beds, between sheets warmed by the brass warming pan that hung on the kitchen wall. I had to climb up into bed, then I sank down and down where every feather whispered rest. But before that we two men made ourselves tidy by washing in the lean-to at the back door, then we departed for a look at the inn.

Hospitality and humour – these are traditions in Farndale, and we of course found both. There were only five customers and one of them was snug in the chimney corner in the shadows. The landlord took him a glass of beer and said, 'You won't know that gentleman?' and pointed to me. An old man's face looked out from the shadows and he said, 'Know 'im? Cause I know 'im! I knew him as soon as he put 'is 'ead inside that door. I knew you when you rode that owd fussock *(donkey)* down to school.' I went over for a chat and found that he had been waggoner for my Uncle Arthur. After a while I filled his glass and rejoined my friend the farmer. I was introduced to the other customers and we settled down to chat about local customs. They still had their hunt, a pack of trencher-fed hounds like the Bilsdale. When the huntsman rides along the valley road and blows his horn down come the light-coloured hounds hell for leather from every farm in the dale.

Suddenly came the voice of the waggoner from the far corner: 'Where aboots are ye living noo? You don't live roond 'ere, do ye?'

'No. I live at Hull.'

To this he commented slowly and sadly, 'My goodness! What a spot!' then sank again into his corner to think. After another ten minutes or so came his second question. 'An' what are ye doing for a livin'? Ah can tell by lookin' at ye that ye're not farming. What sort o' job ha' ye gotten?'

'I'm a teacher,' I said.

There was a full minute's silence then I heard a scornful voice saying, 'Lor', what a come doon!'

Had I been wise I should have said nothing in reply, but I pointed out to him that the education of the rising generation was a vital task *etc. etc.*, to which platitudes he turned a deaf ear and concentrated on his next question. 'Ain't you a headmaster yet?'.

I said that I *was* one and he demanded, 'How many bairns in your school? Is it as big as East Moors? Or is it a big 'un like Helmsley?'

By this time I was getting a little resentful of this public interrogation and thought I would finish it off. 'About seven hundred children.'

That *did* quieten him for a while, then he spoke. 'You've a tidy little flock,' he said, and then he added thoughtfully, 'Them at Carlton Park 'appen 'as seven hundred sheep.'

'What's that got to do with it?' I asked.

The old man laughed heartily and banged his fist on the table. 'E can sell 'is bloomin' sheep whenever 'e wants to!' he said triumphantly, and after this no more was said. He had effectively disposed of me and I shrank visibly. There were times when I would willingly have sold some of my sheep.

Another character engaged my attention, a craftsman who assured me he was eighty-five, though he looked a youngish sixty. I asked him for his recipe. 'I nobbut have two simple rules,' he said. I filled his glass and waited. 'First rule's this: never cross your bridges afore you get to 'em. They'll still be there.'

I had to wait a while and supply a second glass, then he spoke. 'Second rule! Do you drink tea?' I nodded. 'Stop it!' he said.

He disliked modern women, so he said. 'Came up in t'bus yesterday and twenty o' them college women got aboard. That lahtle conductor says to me, "Grandpa, you should stand up an' offer a lady yer seat." "Not ruddy likely," I says. "Them young women smoke like men, they drink like men and they dress like men. They can damn well *stand* like men," I says.'

Next morning I rose early and we soon rounded up the twelve lost sheep. We found them close by, back on their familiar grazing ground on the open moor. Then I said farewell to my host and hostess and the children saw me off at the staggarth yat. Tramping away southward over the heather hills, heading for my little flock on the bank of the Humber, I sang lustily and with good courage. The psalmist was right enough – it is from those well beloved hills that help in abundance comes.

Postscript

Kirkdale House, Huggate.

When he retired, Stephen, typically, was not content to buy a cottage with 'roses round the door'. He moved into a 16-roomed former rectory complete with 2½ acres of garden and paddock at Huggate-on-the-Wolds. This was promply named Kirkdale House and at each sub-sequent removal the oak nameboard that I carved as a present went in the van with the family possessions. Stephen's parents had been married in the tiny Kirkdale Minster near to the cave mentioned in the 'Cave in the Quarry'.

His colleagues, knowing of his desire to return to a rural way of life, included among his retirement presents a piglet. Blue ribbons adorned his neck and tail and 'Percy' as he was immediately named can be seen in the photograph which appeared in the Hull Daily Mail on 29 April, 1955. The crate is surrounded by children who, like Form Four in the first of these stories, were taken for a day on the moors. I believe that,

The presentation of Percy the pig.
(Photograph courtesy of the Hull Daily Mail.*)*

although the children undoubtedly benefited from the day out of school, Stephen arranged these outings with great enthusiasm so that he could escape again to his well beloved hills.